EDEXCEL
BUSINESS *for* GCSE
INTRODUCTION TO ECONOMIC UNDERSTANDING

Jonathan Brook
Jo Farmer
Ian Marcousé

DYNAMIC LEARNING

HODDER
EDUCATION
AN HACHETTE UK COMPANY

Orders: please contact Bookpoint Ltd, 130 Milton Park, Abingdon, Oxon OX14 4SB. Telephone: (44) 01235 827720.
Fax: (44) 01235 400454. Lines are open from 9.00 – 5.00, Monday to Saturday, with a 24 hour message answering service.
You can also order through our website www.hoddereducation.co.uk

If you have any comments to make about this, or any of our other titles, please send them to
educationenquiries@hodder.co.uk

British Library Cataloguing in Publication Data
A catalogue record for this title is available from the British Library

ISBN: 978 1 444 10793 7

First Edition published 2010
Impression number   10 9 8 7 6 5 4
Year   2017   2016   2015   2014

Hachette UK's policy is to use papers that are natural, renewable and recyclable products and made from wood
grown in sustainable forests. The logging and manufacturing processes are expected to conform to the environmental
regulations of the country of origin.

Cover photo © Amanda Rohde/istockphoto.com
Typeset by Servis Filmsetting Ltd, Stockport, Cheshire.
Printed in Dubai for Hodder Education, An Hachette UK Company, 338 Euston Road, London NW1 3BH

Contents

SECTION 1 How can I start thinking like an economist?

SECTION 2 Risk or certainty?

SECTION 3 Big or small?

SECTION 4 Is growth good?

SECTION 5 Is the world fair?

How to use

Edexcel Business for GCSE: Introduction to Economic Understanding introduces students to key economic concepts and provides relevant and interesting case studies to bring the world of economics to life. From a group of surfers highlighting the role of stakeholders in the economy to the issue of global income inequality, this book is packed with useful information and factual nuggets to support students' learning.

The book cuts out unnecessary jargon, pulling out the key terms and putting them into appropriate contexts, making the material accessible and appealing to learners. It is designed to allow students to use economic concepts and economic understanding to challenge their thinking, pose thought-provoking questions and offer solutions to the national and global challenges facing individuals, companies, governments and nations across the world.

Introduction to Economic Understanding begins by introducing students to the foundations of economics; scarcity, value and opportunity cost. It then moves on to look at the role of businesses, challenges in the economy and different government solutions. The final section of the book asks the question 'Is the world fair' and explores global poverty levels, trade and the role of international organisations. Whilst the units follow in a logical order for students and mirror that of the Edexcel GCSE course, each is written to be self-contained, so can be read in any order and 'dipped into' to suit the needs of the learner.

Throughout the book revision terms are highlighted, key information is brought forward, questions are posed about the text and exam-style articles are presented with appropriate questions. Each chapter also suggests some exciting class based activities to support student learning. The text is organised into five key sections:

1. How can I start thinking like an economist?

2. Risk or certainty?

3. Big or small?

4. Is growth good?

5. Is the world fair?

Introduction to Economic Understanding is written to match Unit 5 of the GCSE course from Edexcel. Most of the material, though, can be a huge help in developing the skills needed for OCR and AQA exams.

Jonathan Brook and Josephine Farmer

Acknowledgements

Firstly, we'd both like to thank Ian for the opportunity to get involved in the series and for his support and kind compliments throughout the writing process. We hope you consider the book to be a worthy addition to the series.

Thank you to all the people at Hodder who have worked hard to support us in getting the book to a standard of which we can be proud.

Jon would like to thank all of his students at Droitwich Spa High School who have offered their thoughts on everything from cover design to sentence structure and most things in between. I've written this book with a vision that it will allow you to enjoy learning about economics as much as I enjoy teaching it to you.

Jo would like to thank her current students at Central Technology College, Gloucester as well as her former students at Campion School, Leamington Spa. You have provided me with a forum to test ideas, questions and activities. You inspire great teaching and I hope you and other students find this book supports you on your learning journey.

Jonathan Brook and Josephine Farmer

The authors and publishers would like to thank the following for the use of photographs in this volume:

© Author's Image Ltd/Alamy, p3; © Ray Tang/Rex Features, p10; © Greggs Plc, p29; © Sergey Galushko – Fotolia.com, p34; © Geoff Moore/Rex Features, p46; © Rex Features, p82; © AFP/Getty Images, p89; © Maggie Hardie/Rex Features, p104; Reproduced with kind permission of Marks & Spencer, p110; © Sean Smith/Guardian News & Media Ltd 2009, p123.

The authors and publishers would like to thank the following for permission to reproduce copyright material:

Paint Pots p17; NASA p102; © Copyright 2006 SASI Group (University of Sheffield) and Mark Newman (University of Michigan) p100, p124; World Trade Organization p129.

HOW CAN I START THINKING LIKE AN ECONOMIST?

Scarcity

When your friends ask you if you want to go to the cinema with them, your answer will normally depend on a couple of issues: how much money you have, and if you have enough time after doing other things. If you *do* have enough money and time to get other things done then you'll go to see the latest blockbuster with your friends. If you don't, you'll just have to put up with hearing them talking about the film when you see them next. But what about next time they ask if you want to do something? For example, can you afford to go ice-skating the next day?

The problem is that we tend to have unlimited wants, while at the same time having **scarce resources**. Everyone could write a huge list of the things they'd like to have if they had unlimited resources to buy them with, but unfortunately our resources are scarce.

Everyone (people, businesses and the government) has to make decisions about scarce resources every day. Their decisions obviously won't be about going to the cinema or ice-skating but will involve the same issue of whether they have enough resources to be able to say 'yes'. Everyone is constantly making decisions about how to use their scarce resources in the 'best' way for them.

Resources

A **resource** is anything that allows us to satisfy our unlimited wants. This could be money (as it allows us to buy the resources) or it could be anything else that we could exchange in order to get the resources we want. For example, an IT expert could exchange his knowledge with a friend in return for hiring their holiday home for a reduced rate. An African farmer may exchange one of his donkeys for two goats. In all cases the resources are limited: they are scarce.

So what is economics?

Economics is the study of what goes through people's minds when they are making their decisions about what to do with their scarce resources. Knowing this will give you the power to understand (and even predict) the decisions that people make every day!

Conclusion

People have unlimited wants but because their resources are scarce they have to decide how best to use their resources to get what is 'best' for them.

Talking Point

In a natural disaster such as a hurricane what will be the scarcest resources?

Revision Essentials

Resources – things that are needed in order to satisfy wants, e.g. money, time, staff or land.

Scarce resources – **A situation where there aren't enough resources for everyone to get what they want all of the time.**

Exercises

(A and B: 16 marks; 30 minutes)

A1. Rank the following in terms of their importance to you:

- TV
- water
- hair straighteners
- shelter
- the latest Nike trainers
- food
- cinema tickets
- warmth.

Thinking about your list and any money that you may have, what is meant by scarce resources? (4)

2. Copy and complete the following sentence using the words supplied below. (4)

We have unlimited _____ and _____ resources. A resource could be our own money, or a physical resource such as water. As a result of scarce resources we have to make _____. These have effects on other people, communities and countries.

wants	choices	scarce

B Identify four scarce resources in the photo below and describe why they are scarce. The first one has been done for you. (8)

Example: People could be seen as a resource. They could represent workers. These workers might have important skills that not everyone has. More people might want their skills than the number of them available. This would make them scarce.

Classroom Activity

(Groups of 2 or 3; 30 minutes)

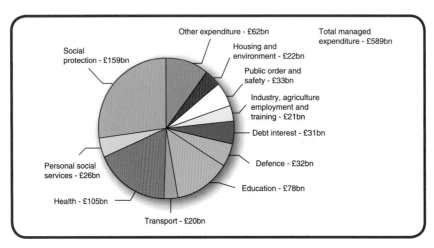

Government expenditure in the UK

Look at the pie chart taken from www.hm-treasury.gov.uk. It shows the projected government expenditure from 2007–08 in the UK.

With a partner, use this information (or similar for any other country) to produce a presentation to summarise how government money is spent in the UK. You need to ensure that you include the terms 'scarcity', 'choice', 'needs' and 'wants' in your presentation.

Practice Questions

Every day NHS managers are dealing with scarce resources. They must decide what is the best way of spending their budgets, and their decisions can have life and death consequences.

Herceptin is a drug that can be used to treat breast cancer and increase life expectancy of sufferers. This drug is estimated to cost £10,000 per patient per year.

Questions

(12 marks; 30 minutes)

1 Explain how the Herceptin case illustrates the concepts of scarcity and choice. (6)

2 Analyse a decision to provide Herceptin to any patients who could benefit from it. (6)

Chapter 2

Value

In August 2007 miners in South Africa claimed to have found a diamond they believed to be twice the size of the existing record-holder, the Cullinan. It was estimated that it would be worth £15m and there would be a huge amount of interest in purchasing it. What does this tell us?

If several people were willing to pay £15m for the diamond it shows us that they **value** the diamond at £15m because they believe they will get £15m worth of satisfaction from owning the diamond (otherwise they wouldn't want to buy it). This value is three times as much as something costing £5m.

Resources and value

Individuals, businesses and the Government will not use their scarce resources unless they believe that what they are giving up is worth as much (i.e. of the same **value**) as what they will be getting in return. When Manchester United accepted £80m for Cristiano Ronaldo in June 2009 they were essentially saying: 'We value Ronaldo at less than £80m.'

Value and satisfaction

Items are valued according to how much **satisfaction** they bring the owner. A person is likely to value an item more highly if he or she will get more satisfaction from it than someone else would. For example, someone working in London may get more satisfaction from going on holiday in the countryside than someone who already lives there, so would value that holiday more. You might also value one piece of art more than another because it will look good next to another one you already have on your wall.

Items that are scarce tend to be of higher value. This is because people get satisfaction from owning something that only a few other people have.

The Science Bit

The amount of money we are willing to give for something is the most common way of demonstrating our valuation of something. Money is a resource itself but also is a means of exchange. It allows us to show our valuations in a way in which everyone can understand (and businesses can respond to).

The Science Bit 2

The amount of satisfaction an item gives us doesn't always have to be constant. Imagine eating piece after piece of chocolate. You won't get anywhere near as much satisfaction from the hundredth piece as you did the first! Your satisfaction is falling with each piece you eat and, as such, so will your valuation.

Conclusion

How highly someone values an item depends on how much satisfaction they think it will bring them. Money is the most common way in which we can demonstrate our valuation of a resource. We will exchange as much money (or other resources) as we think another item (or resource) is worth.

Talking Point

Why do you think diamonds are so 'valuable?'

Revision Essentials

Means of exchange – **a method for allowing transactions to take place, e.g. money or (years ago) gold.**

Satisfaction – **the enjoyment received when consuming a product or service (or resource).**

Value – **the worth of something represented by the amount of money we are prepared to pay for it.**

Exercises

(A and B: 10 marks; 20 minutes)

A Put these in order of their value to you.

Cinema ticket to see the latest blockbuster
A new DVD
A drink in a coffee shop with your friends
£5 top up for your phone
An extra 30 minutes in bed tomorrow morning

Explain how you chose the order. For example, did you order them by how much they would cost you to buy or did you order them in another way? (4)

B In February 2008, famous graffiti artist Banksy sold a canvas called 'Keep it Spotless' for a record $1.9m at a charity auction in New York.

Using the terms 'value' and 'satisfaction', why do you think someone was prepared to spend so much money on this picture? (6)

Classroom Activity

(Groups of 2–4; 30 minutes)

An air crash onto a desert island has left just you and your worst enemy alive. The plane fell into the sea, so there isn't much debris. You are barefoot, with just enough clothing to cover your embarrassment. There is no sign of other people; all you can see is sea and jungle. Between you, all that you now own are the following items:

- a Mach 3 razor

- a pen

- mixed currencies worth £850

- a Ralph Lauren watch

- an iPod Nano

- a pair of trainers

- a pillow

- a bottle of Evian water

- a battered straw hat

- a penknife.

First, individually jot down the order in which you would place these items; you have 10 minutes to do this.

Second, work with your team to decide the three most important items your team would want to keep.

Third, explain this to the class, using the concepts of value and satisfaction.

Practice Questions

British Airways calls itself a 'full-service global airline', offering year-round low fares through a number of well-located airports across the globe.

If you were to try and book a ticket from London to New York for two weeks over the Christmas and New Year period you would pay under £450 in Economy seating and over £2,500 for First Class. In either seat you would depart and arrive at the same time but in First Class you would receive the added extras of flat bed, first-class food and exceptional service.

Questions

(10 marks; 25 minutes)

1 If you paid £2,500 for a First Class seat, describe what this means in terms of value. (3)

2 British Airways sells thousands of First Class seats and even more Economy seats. Use the terms 'value' and 'satisfaction' to explain the sales of both these types of service. (7)

Chapter 3

Opportunity cost

Each year the Chancellor of the Exchequer is responsible for setting the Government's budget for the year ahead. The Chancellor must decide how much to spend on health care, education, defence, law and order, benefits, pensions, transport, housing, etc. Teachers celebrate when he promises to spend more on schools; soldiers want to be fighting with the most up-to-date technology at their disposal.

Teachers, soldiers, doctors and pensioners have unlimited wants but, just like individuals, the government has scarce resources. The Chancellor can't possibly satisfy everybody with his budget. Every pound he spends on extra submarines for the Navy is a pound he could have spent on increasing pensions for the elderly or extra police officers to keep the streets safer.

Scarce resources make **choices** essential. When we make choices we consider the value we have placed on things. Imagine you have £50 and there are two pairs of shoes you like, both priced at £50. Which pair will give you the most satisfaction and you will therefore value the highest?

Assuming you value one pair at least at £50 you will purchase the pair that would give you the highest satisfaction (and therefore the one that you value the highest) and leave the other. But what about the other pair? You have chosen to sacrifice them in preference for something else.

The pair of shoes you left behind is your **opportunity cost.** You have scarce resources and because of this you have given up one thing for another, just like the Chancellor may sacrifice spending on the benefits system in favour of spending on health care. The 'opportunity cost' is the value of the next best alternative that you gave up.

Trade-offs

Economists often refer to sacrifices as **trade-offs**. They try to predict or explain why someone has made a trade-off by investigating their opportunity cost.

For example, James is deciding what to do for his birthday. He has two options: Go-Karting or Paintballing, which he enjoys equally as much. Both parties will cost the same amount of money. Paintballing means that more of his friends can come but his girlfriend, Amber, won't go.

	Go-Karting	Paintballing
James' enjoyment	Equal	Equal
Financial cost	Equal	Equal
Number of friends	10	15
Will Amber come?	Yes	No

James decides to go Go-Karting. What does this say about his valuations? Why has he made such a trade-off? What is his opportunity cost? What is the value of his opportunity cost? Let's work it out.

James' enjoyment of Go-Karting and Paintballing is equal and so is the financial cost. Go-Karting means fewer friends can come but that Amber will come. From this we can work out that James values Amber's presence more than that of five of his other friends so he has traded off five friends for Amber. This can be measured by looking at his opportunity cost, that is:

- five friends
- the chance to go Paintballing.

Conclusion

Scarce resources force us to make choices or trade-offs. The opportunity cost of a trade-off shows how much more we value one thing over another.

Revision Essentials

Choices – decisions that need to be made as a result of having scarce resources.

Opportunity cost – the value of the next best alternative that has been given up.

Trade-off – the item we have to give up in order to get something else.

Exercises

(A and B: 15 marks; 30 minutes)

A1. In your own words describe what is meant by the term opportunity cost. (2)

2. Copy and complete the following table. In the left-hand column give an example of an opportunity cost of making the decision. (4)

Decision	Opportunity cost
Sarah goes into her local newsagent and buys a chocolate bar; this costs her 50p	
A business decides to spend £10,000 on a new advertising campaign	
The Government chooses to spend an additional £2bn on education	
An international charity chooses to spend a proportion of donations on foodstuff and blankets.	

B   *University fees and rising student debt continue to deter some people from going to university and this has now become a political as well as a social issue. A survey of young people in Hull showed that more than half were less likely to apply for university or college because of the introduction of fees.*

Adapted from *The Guardian*, 29 February 2000

1. Evaluate the opportunity costs of going to university. You should consider the costs associated with not going to university: i.e. what might you be giving up? (9)

Classroom Activity

(Groups of 2; 50 minutes)

With a partner, have a look at the Arts Council England's website www.artscouncil.org.uk/ (alternatively your teacher may print out some examples for you). They distribute money from the Government and the National Lottery into the Arts in England.

Produce an information sheet that shows:

● examples of investment in the area of the country where you are that you think has been a good use of funding

● an examination of the opportunity cost of this investment, i.e. in what other areas could the Arts Council have spent the money?

Practice Questions

In October 2008 the Westfield Shopping Centre opened in West London, with 265 shops and 50 restaurants. The building of the centre is estimated to have created 7,000 jobs and brought new transport links. The owners of the shopping centre invested £170m.

The shopping centre has also had some negative impacts. Many of these result from the estimated 70,000 weekend visitors, which has put a strain on parking, public transport and roads. This all has an impact on the local residents in the area.

Westfield Shopping Centre

Questions

(12 marks; 30 minutes)

1 Transport for London (who provide a range of different means of transport in the capital such as buses, the tube and trains) chose to provide £30m of public money to pay for the new transport links. Describe two opportunity costs of this decision. (4)

2 Evaluate how useful the concept of opportunity cost is in helping to make decisions in situations such as the building of a shopping centre. (8)

Price sensitivity and substitutes

The price that is charged for an item affects how much of it people will buy. Generally speaking, if the price goes down more people will buy it and if it goes up the retailer can expect a fall in the number sold.

This is often shown using a 'demand curve' as was shown in Unit 1 of *Edexcel Business for GCSE: Introduction to Small Business*.

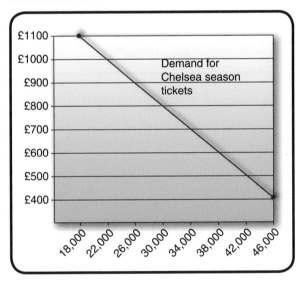

Demand curve

The graph shows that not all Chelsea supporters have £800+ to spend on a season ticket. So the demand curve slopes downwards: the higher the price, the lower the demand.

Demand for Cadbury's Dairy Milk bars will depend on the answer to a number of questions:

● What is the price of Dairy Milk?
● Is the rival brand (such as Galaxy) cheaper?
● Is the product unique?

● Is the product fashionable? (Are consumers worried about their weight?)
● Is it easy to find and buy?
● Is it well promoted and advertised?
● How warm is it outside? (Considerably less chocolate is sold in the summer.)

As a profit-making organisation, Cadbury's will normally seek to make as much profit as possible and try charging more for its products. How much can it get away with charging? The answer depends on the **price sensitivity** of customers.

Sensitivity

How sensitive consumers are to a change in price is dependent on the answers to the above questions. Often the two most important factors are the rival brand's price and whether or not the product is unique.

If a product isn't unique then consumers can easily **substitute** it with a rival, especially if they are similarly priced. Where a product is very unique there are no close substitutes. So a consumer can't substitute one product for another if the price of one increases.

Consider that Galaxy and Dairy Milk are the same price. If Cadbury slightly puts the price of Dairy Milk up and consumers think 'I'm willing to pay a little bit more for Dairy Milk so I'll stick with it' demand isn't sensitive to price. However, the fact that Dairy Milk isn't unique and Galaxy is a close substitute means that consumers will easily be able to switch if the price goes any higher.

	Answer	Sensitivity to price	Answer	Sensitivity to price
Is the rival brand cheaper?	Yes	High	No	Low
Is the product unique?	Yes	Low	No	High
Is the product fashionable?	Yes	Low	No	High
Is it easy to find and buy?	Yes	Low	No	High
Is it well promoted and advertised?	Yes	Low	No	High

Conclusion

The number, price and availability of substitutes (as well as other factors) affect how sensitive consumers are to a change in price. If consumers can't (or don't want to) substitute they will be insensitive to price changes. If they can (and want to) they will be sensitive to price.

Talking Point

Can you think of any products where consumers are particularly price sensitive or insensitive? Why is this?

Revision Essentials

Price sensitivity – how much the demand changes according to a change in the price. Price sensitivity depends on numerous factors, most notably the number, price and availability of substitutes.

Substitute – a rival product that a consumer can switch to if the price of a product changes.

Exercises

(A and B: 16 marks; 30 minutes)

A1. Using soft drinks as an example, describe what is meant by the terms 'substitute' and 'price sensitivity'. (4)

2. Rank these in order of price sensitivity (most sensitive first): (2)

   - *The Sun* newspaper

   - Cadbury's Roses chocolates

   - Versace Jeans

   - petrol

   - a supermarket

3. Reflect on the list you have made and describe why you decided on that order. Try to use the key terms 'substitutes' and 'price sensitivity' in your description. (4)

B *A challenging business environment meant that even in the run up to Christmas in 2008 retailers weren't optimistic. However, bargain and charity shops were busier than normal. In Oxfam sales were up 3.5 per cent on the previous year and the charity was expecting annual profits of £21m.*

   Adapted from *The Guardian,* 3 November 2008

1. State two reasons why people were extra sensitive to price in 2008? (2)

2. Explain the reasons why customers chose to substitute new high-street names for second-hand clothes in Oxfam? (4)

Classroom Activity

(Groups of 2; 20 minutes)

In pairs, make a list of all the products or services that you have spent your money on in the past week.

- First, rank them in order, showing which ones you would be more likely to change if the price increased.

- Now suggest substitutes that you would choose for the top five products or services.

Be ready to share your thoughts with the rest of the class; make sure you use the key terms 'price sensitivity' and 'substitute'.

Practice Questions

The rising cost of fuel

In 2004 the price of crude oil hit a 21-year high. Gordon Brown was pushed by environmental campaigners to increase the price of petrol at the pumps. Campaigners wanted a 1.4p rise per litre of fuel because they argued the tax should reflect the damage motoring causes to the environment.

Adapted from *The Times,* 12 August 2004

Questions

(14 marks; 30 minutes)

1 State whether consumers are price sensitive when it comes to buying fuel. Explain your answer. (6)

2 To what extent do you think it is a good decision to increase the tax on fuel? (8)

Chapter 5

Increasing revenue

In early 2009, Apple announced they would no longer charge a fixed 79p for every single music track on the iTunes Music Store. Instead, they would move to a more flexible system with prices at 59p, 79p and 99p. Would this increase or reduce the company's revenue?

Revenue

Revenue is calculated by multiplying the selling price by the quantity sold:

Revenue = selling price x quantity sold.

Selling price	Quantity sold	Impact on revenue
Up	Same	Up
Same	Up	Up
Up	Down	?
Down	Up	?
Down	Same	Down
Same	Down	Down

As explained in Chapter 4, putting the price of something up is likely to push sales volume down. Even for a hot new computer game, a very high price will stop some fans from being able to afford it. So, what happens to revenue if selling price goes up and quantity sold goes down?

Revenue and price sensitivity

You also know from Chapter 4 that the size of the change in the quantity sold is dependent on how price sensitive consumers are. Sensitivity to price is illustrated by how steep the line is on the demand curve.

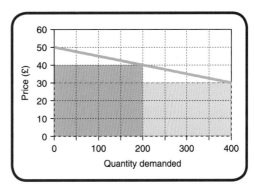

Product A: Demand curve

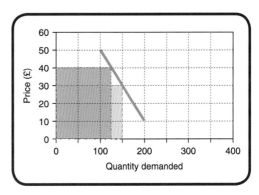

Product B: Demand curve

The shallow demand curve for product A shows consumers are very sensitive to price. At a price of £30 then 400 people want to buy the product, but a price increase to £40 cuts demand to 200 people. So, a £10 increase in price has pushed sales down by a half: from 400 to 200.

For product B the steep line shows customers aren't as sensitive to price; a £10 increase in price from £30 to £40 only stopped 25 customers parting with their money.

The shaded areas in the graphs represent the amount of revenue the product is earning.

For product A:

Revenue = selling price x quantity sold

= £30 x 400

= £12,000

OR

Revenue = selling price x quantity sold

= £40 x 200

= £8,000

For product B:

Revenue = selling price x quantity sold

= £30 x 150

= £4,500

OR

Revenue = selling price x quantity sold

= £40 x 125

= £5,000

For the two different products, increasing price by £10 has had a dramatically different impact on revenue. For product A, the price increase caused revenue to fall by £4,000, while for product B the price increase caused revenue to increase by £500.

Economists found that Apple's strategy of increasing the price of some tracks to 99p has increased its revenue on the top 100 songs. This shows that Apple's customers aren't very price sensitive when it comes to buying digital music.

Adapted from
http://www.billboard.biz

The Science Bit

Often demand curves aren't straight. There are points where customers just can't face paying an extra £1. So the extra penny from £9.99 to £10.00 has a bigger impact on demand than 1p from £9.98 to £9.99 (which is why there are a lot of £9.99 prices in shops).

Conclusion

When changing price, the direction (and extent to which) revenue moves depends on how price sensitive customers are. Businesses must estimate how price sensitive they think their customers are when changing their prices.

Talking Point

Choose *one* of the following products. Do you think that it is highly price sensitive, or not very price sensitive? Explain your reasons.

● a peppermint Aero

● a £180,000 Ferrari

● a kilo of bananas at Tesco.

Revision Essentials

Price sensitivity – **the extent to which demand changes when price changes.**

Revenue – **the money earned from selling products and services. It is calculated by multiplying the selling price by the quantity sold. Whether or not increasing price increases revenue depends on price sensitivity.**

Exercises

(A and B: 22 marks; 40 minutes)

A1. How would a business calculate its revenue? (2)

2. If a hairdresser charges £20 per cut and £40 per colour, how much revenue would they make in a day where they completed four cuts and three colours? (4)

3. Sarah runs a dog-grooming business and has worked out a link between the price she charges and the number of dogs she then has booked in, per day.

Price charged (£)	Number of dogs washed per day
0	20
2	16
4	12
6	8
8	4
10	0

Calculate how much revenue Sarah makes when she charges:

a) £2 per dog

b) £8 per dog. (2)

4. Sarah currently charges £2 per dog and would like to increase her prices. However, she is worried that people will not bring their dogs to her any more and that her revenue will fall. In order to maximise revenue should Sarah increase her price? If so, to what level? (4)

B Kate runs a business called Paint Pots based in Worcester, where customers purchase a piece of pottery that hasn't been painted or glazed and add their own designs using different paints. The pottery is then fired in their kiln and collected by the customer. When Kate took over the business she found out that the previous owner charged low prices for the unfired pottery but then charged again for the paints and the firing service. Kate decided to charge a one-off fee per item painted and fired.

Kate isn't sure whether this was a good plan.
(Example based on http://www.paintpotsworcester.co.uk/)

1. Describe what Kate could do to find out whether her revenue increased. (4)

2. Kate believes that customers are becoming increasingly price sensitive and is considering reducing her prices. How will she know whether this is a good idea? (6)

Classroom Activity

(Groups of 3–4; 50 minutes)

You will be given a menu of different fruit juices and their prices. You will also be given a team budget. Your team needs to design three fruit cocktails, purchase the ingredients displayed on the menu and then work together to make the drinks.

Once you have done this, you need to choose a price for each of your drinks.

For round one, your classmates will then move around the room (your group too) deciding on which drinks they would like to buy; they can purchase up to 100 for their new restaurant but they must fill in an order sheet. This means you need to think carefully about how sensitive your customers (your classmates) are to price. (Don't forget the competition either!)

In round two, look at the order sheets from round one. Now have a go at changing your prices and repeat round one, with other teams having another £100 to spend. What happens to your orders as a result of the price change?

Look at the order sheets from both rounds. Have a conversation with your team about what happened to your revenue from round one to round two. Next, see what happened to other teams' orders. Does this help to explain the changes in your revenue?

Practice Questions

Customers who travel on some of the busiest of Britain's commuter routes are angry as train operators have increased fares by up to 15%. On top of this, customers argue that they put up with overcrowding and poor customer service. Passenger Focus, the rail users' watchdog has described the situation as 'unjustified and unfair'.

For example, an annual ticket from Canterbury to London will increase by over £300.

Adapted from *The Guardian*, 1 January 2008

Questions

(12 marks; 25 minutes)

1 Consider the comment that the price rise is 'unfair'. How sensitive do you think rail commuters are to increases in price? Explain your answer. (6)

2 To what extent do you feel the revenues of train operators will be affected by the price rise? (6)

Do all stakeholders have the same perspective?

Conflicting stakeholders

In 2005 an organisation called 'Plane Stupid' was formed with the aim of controlling the growth of air travel in the UK. It has since protested, sometimes illegally, at three airports and the Houses of Parliament. The members wanted to draw attention to their belief that air travel is a major contributor to climate change. Meanwhile, owners of airports and airlines hope for continuing growth in air travel as it brings them increased profits.

Different perspectives

Plane Stupid and airport owners are **stakeholders** because they have an interest in the actions and success of air-travel business. However, different stakeholders often have different perspectives on an issue.

Stakeholder	Perspective on airport expansions	Reason
Plane Stupid (and other pressure groups)	Negative	Believe air travel is already excessively contributing to climate change
Shareholders of the airports and airlines	Positive	Expansion would bring them higher revenues and profits
Workers at airports and on airlines	Positive	Expansion will bring increased job security
Travellers	Positive	New facilities are more appealing and reduce delays from overcrowding of runways and terminals
Government	Positive	Expansion would encourage international travellers to holiday and do business in Britain
Local residents/environment	Negative	Expansion will create noise and air pollution that will damage habitats and may reduce house prices

Clearly there are **conflicts of interest** between stakeholders where the issue of airport expansion is concerned. Some stakeholders are in favour of airport expansion, while some aren't – often for different reasons.

Stakeholder conflicts aren't restricted to airport expansion. There are lots of common areas where stakeholders have different perspectives on the actions of a business:

- Shareholders may force managers to cut corners in order to get maximum profits while consumers want safe, reliable products and workers want to work without fear of injury or harm for a fair wage.

- The government may want more nuclear power plants to decrease our dependence on foreign gas and coal but local residents may be frightened of the risk of leaks of radioactive materials.

- Drugs companies want to charge high prices for medicines to repay their investment in research, while pressure groups would like to see medicines being sold much more cheaply in developing countries to prevent disease and death.

Stakeholder power

How these conflicts are resolved depends on the relative **power** of the stakeholder. Stakeholder power comes from how **influential** the stakeholder is. If workers have specific skills that make them scarce and difficult to replace, they are influential and have power. The business must respect their views in case they decide to leave.

Meanwhile, if the local residents of a polluting company are not its customers they will carry little influence unless they have the power to disrupt production.

Conclusion

A business will have several stakeholders interested in its actions and success. The extent to which a business considers each stakeholder's perspective will be based around how influential and powerful the stakeholder is.

Talking Point

Are businesses that claim to be considerate of their stakeholders doing so because they genuinely 'care', or is it because they want to be looked upon favourably by their customers?

Revision Essentials

Conflict of interest – **where different groups of stakeholders each have a different perspective on an issue.**

Power and influence of the stakeholder – **some stakeholders are more influential in the decision-making of a business than others.**

Stakeholder – **an individual, group or organisation that is interested in the actions and success of a business.**

Exercises

(A and B: 17 marks; 35 minutes)

A1. State three stakeholders for your local convenience store. (3)

2. Describe a situation where the three stakeholders might disagree with each other. (4)

3. Describe a situation where the three stakeholders might share the same point of view. (4)

B   In August 2009 BAA announced new plans for a £1bn upgrade of Terminal 2 at Heathrow Airport. This is part of a much bigger expansion of Heathrow and has been met with resistance from campaigners.

Using your knowledge about stakeholders and their different viewpoints, what could Heathrow Airport do to try to bring the stakeholders' views closer together? (6)

Classroom Activity

(Groups of 5; 30 minutes)

There are many stakeholders in the relocation of a school

Imagine that your school is going to be re-built. The plan is to sell your school site to a large supermarket and, using the money, relocate the school three miles away on a slightly smaller site.

You need to work in groups of 5. Each of you should take the role of a different stakeholder. You have 10 minutes to decide whether you want the school to move and prepare your arguments ready to present your case.

Once you have done this, work as a group to decide whether some of the stakeholders have more power than others. Who do you think would have most influence over the decision, and why?

Practice Questions

When the government announced ten pro-posed sites for Britain's first 'eco-towns' there were widespread protests. Over 30 per cent of the houses would be 'affordable housing' and would be a more green way of living. Together these will help to enable Britain to meet its target of building three million homes by 2020.

These plans have divided stakeholders' opinion.

Questions

(16 marks; 35 minutes)

1 Identify four key stakeholders involved in the story above. (4)

2 Choose two of these stakeholders and briefly describe their point of view. (6)

3 Which stakeholder do you feel would be most influential? Explain your answer. (6)

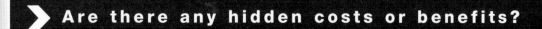

Chapter 7

Positive and negative externalities

Lauren's thoughts about whether or not to drive to work show us how she will make the choice:

1. What satisfaction will I get from driving to work?

2. How much do I value the satisfaction of driving to work?

3. OK ... So how much does driving to work cost?

4. Does driving to work cost more or less than I value it?

Lauren will only drive to work if:

- she values driving at least as much as the cost of driving; and

- there are no alternatives for her that have a smaller opportunity cost.

Individuals and businesses are constantly making decisions and choices. Every decision or choice that they make is made in order to provide them with the most satisfaction they can get for a given cost. Essentially, businesses and individuals act in ways to maximise their own satisfaction for the minimum of opportunity cost.

Lauren, however, has not considered if her choice has any hidden costs or benefits to others (those people referred to in Chapter 6 as stakeholders), such as the local community and local businesses. The costs or benefits to these stakeholders are called **externalities.**

Negative externalities

Lauren's choice to drive to work results in private costs to her such as petrol, road tax and car insurance. However, her choice has costs to stakeholders other than Lauren so her choice has **negative externalities.** There are costs to stakeholders on top of Lauren's prime costs of motoring.

The costs to stakeholders are:

- congestion (slower traffic means deliveries take longer and customers are put off visiting towns so businesses lose out)

- air pollution (including global warming), and

- noise.

As long as Lauren does not have to pay for her negative externalities she will continue to drive to work and her choices will mean that the stakeholders continue to lose out as costs go on unpaid for.

Some stakeholders will lose out more than others, depending on the situation. The choice to smoke a cigarette will have private costs to the smoker such as the price of the cigarette and the deterioration in their own health. The value of the externalities will differ from stakeholder to stakeholder. The NHS may need to pay several thousand pounds for treatment of the smoker due to smoking-related illness over a period of

Congestion will have a cost for stakeholders

time, while a passer-by may only need to pay once for extra dry cleaning after getting the smoke on their clothes.

Positive externalities

Sometimes choices made by individuals or businesses can have benefits for stakeholders other than the decision-maker. For example, the choice by a homeowner to re-paint the outside of their house and keep their garden looking beautiful will, of course, bring them private value and satisfaction. It will also please their neighbours, who will benefit from looking at the garden and the increase in their own house price now that they are no longer next to a scruffy-looking house. This choice has **positive externalities.**

The Science Bit

If the value of negative externalities can be measured (or estimated), governments should be able to impose a tax on the activities. For example, the UK Government taxes cigarettes heavily, which makes sure that smokers are the ones who pay for the extra pressure they place on the NHS.

Conclusion

Economists assume that individuals and businesses act to maximise their own satisfaction and do not consider the cost of their actions on other stakeholders. In a fair world, individuals and businesses would pay for their negative externalities and be rewarded for their positive ones.

Talking Point

Measuring externalities is often problematic. They are hard to quantify using money. How could you put a value on the effects of passive smoking?

Revision Essentials

Negative externality – a cost inflicted on other stakeholders when an individual or business makes a choice.

Positive externality – a benefit shared by other stakeholders when an individual or business makes a choice.

Exercises

(15 marks, 20 minutes)

1. Use an example to help describe what is meant by the following:

   a) Negative externalities (3)

   b) Positive externalities. (3)

2. Identify three stakeholders who would be negatively affected by the planned expansion of Heathrow Airport. (3)

3. Choose the stakeholder who you feel would be the most severely affected by the expansion and explain the negative externalities they face. (4)

4. Describe one way in which the management of Heathrow Airport can act to reduce the negative externalities without cancelling their plans for a third runway. (2)

Classroom Activity

(Groups of 2–4, 20 minutes)

> In the UK, the flu vaccine is being offered to all those aged 65 years and over, people with certain long-term medical conditions, health and social care workers, and those who work in close contact with poultry. In 2002 US researchers recommended the vaccine should be available to all.

Working in groups, produce a three-minute presentation to the rest of the group about the introduction of the flu vaccine in the UK. The presentation should cover the following areas:

- the reasons for the introduction of the vaccine
- an examination of the positive externalities that occur as a result of the flu vaccine on at least two stakeholder groups
- a justified recommendation to the NHS for whether they should provide a free-of-charge vaccine for all. (Try to incorporate in your recommendation the key terms from this chapter and the idea of opportunity cost from Chapter 3.)

The following websites will provide support:

- www.immunisation.nhs.uk
- www.bbc.co.uk.

Practice Questions

A Chocolate Tax?

In March 2009 Dr David Walker suggested to MPs that chocolate should be taxed because he believes that the UK faces a 'diabetic time bomb'. (For further details see: http://news.scotsman.com/latestnews/We-need-a-heavy-tax.5040174.jp.)

The choice to eat lots of chocolate can lead to negative externalities

Questions

(15 marks; 35 minutes)

1 Which two of the following effects can be classed as negative externalities? (2)

- increased levels of violence in city centres over the Christmas period fuelled by greater alcohol consumption

- the reduction in cases of mumps as a result of a vaccine being introduced in the UK in 1988

- the pollution at Colin Glen River in 2008 by the Northern Ireland Water company following an overflow in their waste water treatment works in dry weather

- the improvement in lung functions of bar workers in San Francisco eight weeks after the introduction of a smoking ban in 1998.

2 State two negative externalities that result from the choice to eat large quantities of chocolate. (2)

3 Chose one of your answers from above and explain why the term 'negative externality' can be used to describe this effect. (3)

4 Identify two stakeholders that would be affected by the increase in chocolate consumption in the UK. For each stakeholder, explain how they would be either negatively or positively affected. (8)

Chapter 8

Measuring success

The saying 'revenue is vanity, profit is sanity and cash is king' is often repeated by entrepreneurs, and has frequently made its way into discussions in the TV programme *Dragons' Den*. The Dragons are trying to explain that without cash steadily coming in to pay the bills in a business there may be no business at all tomorrow. They are also saying that they believe that having high revenue may look good but if it's all eaten away by costs there is little to shout about.

The saying includes three of the five methods that are commonly used to measure the success of business.

Ways to measure business success

- **Survival.** A new business may consider it a success simply to have survived the first few years of trading. This period is a steep learning curve and 50 per cent of new businesses fail within the first three years. Managing cash to make sure there is enough to pay the bills is the biggest part of surviving.

- **Revenue.** Revenue is the money coming into a business from customers. In 2008–09 British Airways' revenue was £8,992m, while EasyJet's (2008) was £2,363m. Looking at these figures you could say that British Airways was more successful.

- **Profit.** Profit is what is left of revenue after costs have been paid. In 2008–09 British Airways' profit was –£220m (a loss), while EasyJet (2008) recorded a profit of £123m, making EasyJet the more successful.

- **Market share.** When Toyota overtook General Motors in terms of the number of worldwide car sales, it began to have a larger **market share.** Toyota considered this a great success, having had it as an objective for several years.

- **Corporate social responsibility.** The owners of some organisations consider their businesses to be successful if they have a positive impact on society around them. Some businesses such as Innocent Drinks do this indirectly by donating a percentage of profit to charity. The Co-op does it by trying hard to get its food supplies from Fairtrade sources. Both consider their commitment to society to be a way in which to measure their success.

The Science Bit

Taking figures at face value is a risky business. While EasyJet made more profit than British Airways in 2008–09 they may not in fact consider that to be much of a success given that it represented a 36 per cent fall in profit compared with the previous year. A business may consider an upward trend a relative success, even if it doesn't stack up to the competition. Similarly, it may consider a downward trend a failure even if it is still ahead of its rivals.

Conclusion

There are various methods of measuring the success of a business. The reality is that those who are judging the success of a business would rarely use just one method. Instead they will often use several to evaluate the performance of a business.

Talking Point

Organisations owned and run by the Government often have very different ways of measuring their performance. Can you think of any ways to measure the success of a school? Or a hospital?

Revision Essentials

Market share – a company's sales as a percentage of the entire sales in a particular market.

Profit – what revenue is left after costs have been paid.

Exercises

(A and B: 35 marks; 50 minutes)

A1. State how to calculate the profit made by a business. (2)

2. Describe the meaning of 'market share'. (2)

3. Businesses that have a large market share have higher profits. Do you agree with this statement? Explain your answer. (4)

4. Describe two other ways in which a business can measure its success. (4)

5. Evaluate the effectiveness of any two ways of measuring business success. (6)

B. 2009 saw contrasting reports in terms of business profits. Cadbury reported that profits would be higher than expected, with sales of chocolate up 10 per cent. However, Inchcape, a car dealership, saw a 22 per cent drop in sales over six months and profits slipping.

1. If you were providing a report to the shareholders of Inchcape, describe which other measures you could try to use in order to demonstrate business success. (5)

2. To what extent do you think that shareholders in a business are concerned about corporate social responsibility? (6)

3. Analyse the reasons why Cadbury and Inchcape might report such different levels of success during the same time period. (6)

Classroom Activity

(Groups of 3–4; 30 minutes)

You will be given the name of a business that you will have heard of. You need to produce a short report to hand in to your shareholders (another team), which outlines the success of the business.

Hint: think about how you measure success and what they will want to hear!

Practice Questions

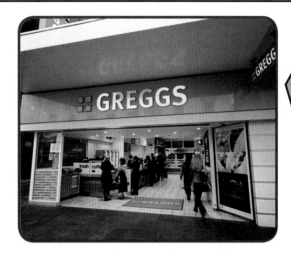

In 2009 Greggs' sales rose by over 4 per cent and profits increased to £16.5m, compared with £15.4m in the first six months of 2008.

Greggs sell 2m sausage rolls and 2.5m sandwiches each week and while these products continue to do well, new product sales have tripled. Meanwhile the cost of ingredients has risen.

Greggs are planning to open 40 new shops in the next six months and are looking to expand their market share. One area they are now looking at is expanding into petrol station forecourts and they are currently trialling this idea.

Despite these successes there are still concerns for the second half of the year; poor summer weather has meant that sales over the past few weeks have been flat compared to last year.

Adapted from: *The Times*, 12 August 2009

Questions

(12 marks; 25 minutes)

1 The article mentions increased costs faced by Greggs. What effect will this have on profits? (2)

2 Faced with increased costs, explain two things that Greggs may do to ensure that their profits will still increase. (4)

3 When Ken McMeikan became Greggs' chief executive in 2008 he planned to increase the work Greggs do with the community. This included children's breakfast clubs and charity giving. He also planned to reduce food waste.

   Explain how Ken's plans might affect Greggs' profits. (6)

Chapter 9

Gaining competitive advantage

In the run-up to Christmas in the early 1990s children tried to persuade their parents to buy them a Nintendo Entertainment System to play the latest computer games on the home television. By 2001 consoles from Nintendo and Sega were rarely found on Christmas lists. Instead, consoles from Microsoft (the original Xbox) and Sony (the Playstation 2) were the ones people wanted. Nintendo's GameCube was a failure. Yet by 2006 Nintendo was unable to meet demand for its new Wii console, with shops regularly selling out due to its huge success.

Console manufacturers will look for ways to gain compeitive advantage

This story of console manufacturers constantly overtaking each other in terms of sales shows how businesses can gain (and re-gain) **competitive advantage** over each other.

What is competitive advantage and why is it important?

Competitive advantage is a term used to describe any factors that help a business succeed when competing with a rival. For example, Apple has a competitive advantage because it has a selection of highly talented product designers and engineers that allows them to create clever products that people enjoy using. AMT Coffee has a competitive advantage in several shopping centres, train stations and airports because they are located in the most convenient place for passers-by in a rush.

How to gain competitive advantage

Competitive advantage can be gained in various ways.

● **Customer research.** Spending time and money on understanding customer needs will mean a business can develop products that customers love, instead of just want. If customers want style, you must work hard to be stylish but if they want value for money, you must compromise. If you don't know what people want, you will never have an edge over your rivals.

- **Being creative.** Using and developing technology can be extremely useful in getting ahead of rivals. Nintendo successfully used existing technology in its Wii remotes to create a new gaming experience that appealed to a wider audience of potential gamers.

- **Cost control.** Businesses who are able to negotiate a better price from suppliers will be able to pass on their savings to customers, meaning they can always win battles based on low prices. Tesco have ruthlessly cut the prices paid to its suppliers in an attempt to gain an advantage over Asda and Sainsbury's.

- **Leadership** Clever business leaders will make sure that their business is quick to react to changes. Changes in the economy or in fashion and tastes may mean that new opportunities crop up that can be exploited. Businesses that respond quickly will seize competitive advantage.

Conclusion

Businesses that can gain competitive advantage have the ability to persuade customers to use their products and services rather than those of their rivals. This makes it much easier to survive in a tough business world. Woolworths was a perfect example of a chain of shops with no obvious competitive advantage. Competitive advantage can be gained in a variety of ways, including research and development, control of costs or skillful management of resources. Great companies, such as Coca-Cola or Honda, manage to sustain a competitive advantage over many years.

Talking Point

How important do you think creativity is when trying to gain a competitive advantage?

Revision Essentials

Competitive advantage – **any factor that helps a business succeed when fighting against a direct rival.**

Exercises

(A and B: 13 marks; 30 minutes)

A1. Explain how having a competitive advantage could lead to business success. (4)

B   The Flower Shop is a florist based in Lindley, West Yorkshire. Owned and run by Helen, a flower fanatic, the Flower Shop caters for a range of occasions as well as making arrangements to order. The shop prides itself on its trendy designs and high-quality service.

Since opening, the Flower Shop has been a huge success and has developed a first-class reputation within the area.

1. Describe how Helen has created a competitive advantage. (3)

2. To what extent do you think offering arrangements made to order is a good strategy for a florist? (6)

Classroom Activity

(Groups of 2; 25 minutes)

When applying for jobs, individuals often try to give themselves a competitive advantage over other applicants.

You have read an advert that is asking for a Saturday helper at a local restaurant. The advert does not say quite what the job would involve, nor does it say how much you are likely to be paid.

> ### Saturday staff wanted at Salvatore's Restaurant, High Street
>
> Do you have the necessary skills to work in our successful Italian restaurant? If so, we need you.
>
> So if you think you are who we are looking for, pop in and speak to **Megan**.

In pairs, put together a short selling pitch to persuade the owner (your teacher) why one of you should be given the job. How are you going to have an advantage over the competition (your other classmates)?

Practice Questions

ASOS.com (As Seen On Screen) was established in June 2000 and is the UK's largest independent online fashion and beauty retailer. With over 35,000 branded and own label products available and 1,500 new lines added each week, ASOS.com is rapidly becoming the market leader in the UK online fashion world.

ASOS is targetted at 16 to 34 year olds and caters for them with a range of women's fashion, menswear, kidswear, accessories and beauty products. Their ranges are huge, with prices of handbags from £12 to £525. With 2.4 million registered users and 5.4 million unique visitors each month, business is booming and they now employ over 250 people. Revenue for 2008–09 stood at over £165m.

ASOS continues to add new lines, provides newsletters and magazines to customers and has recently introduced a new section to their site 'ASOS life'.

Recognising that if you buy online you cannot try the garments on, ASOS has invested heavily in its website and customer service, with many people ready to answer your call if you have a problem.

Source: www.asos.com

Questions

(16 marks; 30 minutes)

1 What evidence is there that ASOS has followed a strategy based on:

   a) creativity? (3)

   b) reducing costs? (3)

2 What do you think is the main reason for ASOS' success? (You may want to go to the website for more information.) (6)

3 Describe two ways in which ASOS could maintain its competitive advantage in the future. (4)

Chapter 10

Losing competitiveness

In the early 1990s Polaroid's worldwide sales topped $2bn. Customers were willing to pay for special cameras and films that instantly processed photographs into paper prints. By 2001, losses forced Polaroid into successive financial difficulties and by 2008 the company had to admit there was no longer a demand for its products. Polaroid stopped producing cameras and films in 2008.

Polaroid cameras lost their competitiveness

The increased competition from one-hour photo developing centres and then from cheaper digital cameras meant that Polaroid could no longer compete; it had lost its competitiveness.

What causes a loss of competitiveness?

- **Losing understanding of customer needs** Businesses that lose sight of what their customers want today and in the future really struggle to stay competitive. The product may be appealing but it may not be affordable for the target market, or not available in the right places. Another possibility is that the price

might be competitive but the product may not have up-to-date features.

- **Loss of productivity** Over time a business can lose control of how productive it is. When businesses get bigger they may find it difficult to stay efficient as they struggle to communicate with and organise a huge workforce. In 2009, the US giant General Motors had to be rescued from bankruptcy. It had been struggling for years to keep up with smaller, sharper competitors such as BMW and Honda.

- **Increased competition** A rival may develop a unique feature that is the new 'must-have' or may start attracting customers with a similar product for a lower price. When either of these things happen, the competition will tempt customers away from the market leader, showing that they are losing their competitiveness.

- **Changing market conditions** With a struggling economy there is reduced demand so businesses find it more difficult to survive. Some businesses find it much more difficult to adapt. A business that fails to understand customer needs when money is tight will be less competitive than one that adapts to the changing market around them.

What happens when you lose competiveness?

- **Reduced profit** When a business is faced with reduced sales and/or increased costs it will struggle to make as much profit as it used to. Lower profits mean less money to invest in upcoming projects, which can damage future competitiveness even further.

- *Damage to reputation* When brand image is very important to sales, being seen as inferior by customers (even for a short while) can be very damaging for future sales.

- *New strategy* One effect of losing competitiveness is that the business will try to develop a new strategy to regain competitive advantage again. Research and investigating will try to pinpoint where competitiveness was lost so that the business can make changes to their current business plan.

- *Closure* An extended period of being uncompetitive will mean that instead of reduced profits the business will begin to make a loss and be forced to close, often leaving debts behind.

Conclusion

Businesses work incredibly hard to gain a competitive advantage so they can be more successful than their rivals. This advantage is difficult to keep hold of. One business's success means others are constantly seeking ways to be even better and collect the rewards for being the market leader. Businesses that lose their advantage struggle with falling profits and a declining reputation, and face closure unless they can come up with a new strategy to get them back on top.

Talking Point

Dragons' Den's Theo Paphitis specialises in transforming businesses that have become uncompetitive and restoring their competitive advantage. What skills do you think Theo has that make him so successful in doing this?

Exercises

(A and B: 20 marks; 40 minutes)

A1. State two ways in which a business can gain competitive advantage. (2)

2. Explain how poor understanding of customer needs could cause a business to lose its competitive advantage. (4)

3. How might a business lose competitive advantage as a result of changing market conditions? (4)

B In an interview Arsene Wenger, Arsenal Football Club's Manager, was asked about the upcoming football season. He said that he believed Aston Villa, a Premiership competitor, would be the big challenger to teams at the top of the league.

1. Arsene Wenger is explaining how Aston Villa could be a team to challenge Arsenal this season. Explain how his thoughts demonstrate the concept of competitive advantage. (4)

2. To what extent do you think that competition is a significant factor in companies losing competitive advantage? Use at least one business example to illustrate your answer. (6)

Classroom Activity

(Groups of 2–4; 45 minutes)

Choose a business with which you are familiar that has experienced problems recently. This could be falling revenues, profits, market share, etc. In your teams, produce a short, one-page summary that includes the following:

- information about the business
- information about the problems the business has experienced
- analysis of the reasons why the business has experienced a decline.

Practice Questions

Early in 2009 the Irish Broadcaster Setanta was forced to stop broadcasting, as it failed to make payments to a number of suppliers. Two hundred employees faced immediate redundancy, and 2.5 million UK viewers were left without compensation for their subscriptions.

The Chairman of Setanta, Sir Robin Miller, explained to *The Telegraph* that, 'Unfortunately, in a difficult and highly competitive market, and despite efforts by the board and management, it has not been possible to find enough funding in the time available to ensure our survival.'

Adapted from *The Telegraph*, 24 June 2009

Giles Smith, a journalist for The Times believed a basic problem with Setanta's strategy was the reason for its failure. He said Setanta's 'timid mission was to look exactly like Sky Sports, but with a lot more yellow on the studio walls.'

Adapted from *The Times*, 13 August 2009

Questions

(10 marks; 25 minutes)

1 Use the articles to explain two reasons why Setanta lost its competitiveness. (4)

2 To what extent do you think that other factors could have had an impact on Setanta's success? (6)

Chapter 11

The importance of cash flow

When Callum, a small builder in Worcester was given the go-ahead to build a house for a customer for £125,000 he was delighted. He knew the house would only cost £100,000 to build, leaving him with a potential £25,000 profit. He persuaded the customer to pay a deposit of £50,000, with the balance of £75,000 due when the house was completed.

Callum went away and bought materials with the deposit and began building the house. However, in the end he wasn't able to finish the house because he had spent all the deposit on materials and had no **cash** left over.

- **Cash** means how much money the business has in the bank (i.e. available) *at a point in time.*

- **Cash flow** is how much money is flowing in and out of a business.

- **Profit** is how much money the business makes after it has paid its costs *over a period of time.* It must not be confused with cash.

Callum knew building the house would bring profit over a period of time. However, he was unable to finish it because he had run out of cash at a point in time along the building process. This was a result of his poor cash flow management meaning the house could never be finished.

What happens when you run out of cash?

Without cash, bills and staff simply cannot be paid – and staff won't return to work on Monday if they weren't paid last week. Telling your suppliers you can't afford to pay for the last delivery means that they are unlikely to send you another. Without staff and stock you'll struggle to get any more cash flowing in.

Unpaid suppliers and workers may take steps to recover their losses in court and you may be closed down. Even if this doesn't happen, the lack of new stock to sell (and staff to sell it) will force the business to shrink and perhaps close.

Why do cash flow problems occur?

There are four reasons why a profitable business may run out of cash:

- Seasonal sales in a business such as an ice-cream shop mean that the summer months make the whole year profitable, but for many months little money will flow in to deal with unexpected costs.

- Late-paying customers delay money coming into the business. Their custom may be profitable but if they don't pay quickly it can cause real problems, especially if they are a big customer.

- A long time taken in production means that it can take a while between having to pay for materials and getting paid for the final product.

- Large start-up costs mean that money is leaving the business really quickly before any customers come through the door.

Conclusion

How businesses manage their cash day to day is more important than worrying about how much profit they will make over the year. Without cash to keep it running, the business won't even have a chance to make a profit. Cash-flow problems occur in seasonal businesses, start-ups and when customers don't pay on time. Businesses must manage these issues effectively in order to avoid business failure.

Talking Point

How might a business encourage its customers to pay on time?

Revision Essentials

Cash – the money the firm holds in notes and coins and in its bank accounts.

Cash flow – the movement of money into and out of the firm's bank accounts.

Exercises

(A and B: 18 marks; 35 minutes)

A1. In business terms, state how cash is different to profit? (2)

2. State what is meant by the term 'cash flow'? (2)

3. Explain why cash flow is important to the success of a business. (4)

B   In November 2008 MFI, the UK's biggest furniture retailer, collapsed. Twenty-six stores closed immediately and 1,000 jobs were lost. In a statement MFI explained that they had suffered from severe cash flow difficulties.

1. Explain how cash flow pressures may have led to the collapse of MFI. (4)

2. To what extent do you believe cash flow was to blame for MFI's closure? What other factors could be considered? (6)

Classroom Activity

(Groups of 2; 30 minutes)

In 2009 Electrolux, the world's second-largest home-appliance manufacturer, said that they expected to see cash flows remaining positive over the coming year. This was in stark contrast to Woolworths, who closed their doors the year before, crippled by £385m debt and a cash flow crisis.

In your pairs produce a mind map highlighting the benefits to a business of a strong cash flow and the difficulties facing a business with poor cash flow.

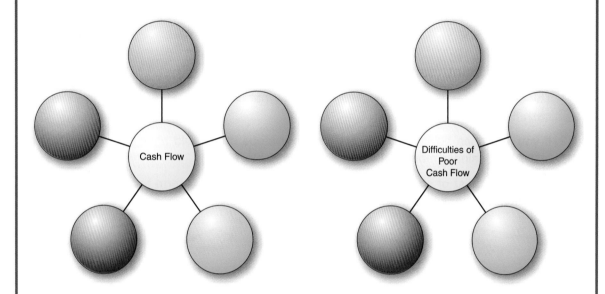

Mind maps

Consider what a business with cash can do, and what a business with no cash is unable to do.

Practice Questions

Can Zavvi be Zaved?

On Thursday 8 January 2009 Zavvi announced the closure of 22 of its stores, with 178 people losing their jobs. This left 92 stores still open, but with the threat of closure hanging over them. A total of 3,200 more jobs would be lost if Zavvi closed down completely.

Zavvi was formed in September 2007. Before that, the stores had traded as Virgin Megastores. In the year to March 2006 the chain made losses of £82m. In 2007 losses were around £50m. The chain's senior managers had the confidence to buy the business from Virgin – helped by being paid £20m to take the business off Virgin's hands. They renamed the stores Zavvi, but lacked the cash to be able to make many other changes. Zavvi continued to sell CDs and DVDs in high street stores. The business was hit in late 2008 by the collapse of Woolworth's music distribution business, which supplied Zavvi with its CDs and DVDs.

In 2008 DVD sales rose by 1.9 per cent, but CD album sales fell 3.2 per cent for the industry as a whole. Considering that online sales grew rapidly, high street stores saw their sales plummet.

Questions

(13 marks; 25 minutes)

1 The article states that Zavvi 'lacked finance'. What do you think this means in terms of cash flow? (3)

2 If you had been advising Zavvi, suggest four steps they could have taken in order to make the business more competitive and profitable. (4)

3 Look at your list of steps and remove any that require short-term investment. Explain the impact of cash flow problems on Zavvi. (6)

RISK OR CERTAINTY?

Chapter 12

Changing demand

In 2008 an event known as the 'credit crunch' moved the UK economy into difficulty. Banks had mismanaged their lending and were unable to continue funding new projects and spending. Businesses became unsure about the future and whether or not workers' jobs were safe. Many thousands of workers did lose their jobs as businesses cut back. Even workers who kept their jobs were nervous about what lay ahead. As a result, consumers reduced their spending dramatically – especially on luxuries. This created even more difficulty for businesses, as they had to deal with **changing demand.**

increased they refer to it as 'positive **economic growth**': demand has increased. When demand is decreasing it is called 'negative economic growth'. Before the credit crunch, the last time this happened was in 1991 – see the graph below.

The Science Bit

Graphs showing economic growth often catch students out. When the line is moving downward (e.g. between 2001 and 2002) it doesn't mean that there is decreasing demand. Instead, it means that demand is increasing but at a *slower rate* than previously. Only when economic growth is less than zero (e.g. 1991) is demand actually decreasing. Demand increasing at a slower rate is troublesome for businesses, but nowhere near as much as decreasing demand.

Economic growth

Over time, the economy goes through cycles of increasing and decreasing demand. Economists measure the value of all the items purchased in the economy over a period of time. If the value has

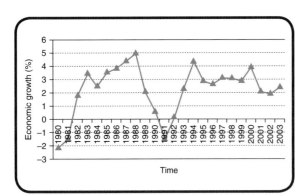

Changes in demand over time
Source: Figures taken from
www.measuringworth.org

What does changing demand mean for businesses?

1. Increasing demand

When the demand in an economy is increasing businesses are generally upbeat as there is more consumer spending to compete for.

Not all businesses benefit, however. Can you imagine your family buying more baked beans because Dad has just got a pay rise? Instead, people substitute 'normal' goods for ones of higher quality. Flushed with a pay rise, someone might buy an Audi instead of a Ford.

2. Decreasing demand

When demand is decreasing the opposite occurs. In extreme cases, people may stop spending completely on luxuries such as holidays or eating out. In practice, however, people find cheaper alternatives. Domino's Pizza reported increased profits when the economy fell away in 2008. People ate less at restaurants and opted for takeaway pizza instead.

Smaller businesses are much more exposed to changes in demand. They often have little cash in reserve to weather the storm of decreasing demand. Fortunately, they are also well placed to react quickly to increasing demand.

Are changes in demand predictable?

Economists, such as those working for the government, regularly try to predict whether demand will increase or decrease in the future.

A forecast of increasing demand for the next three years may persuade Nokia to invest heavily in technology to produce a sophisticated new phone to appeal to consumers willing to spend large amounts of money. If Nokia don't invest, Sony Ericsson might do and take a large amount of market share with a successful new product.

However, quite simply, forecasting the economy is incredibly difficult. This means that any business that bases its strategy around an economic forecast is taking a risk that the forecast will turn out to be inaccurate. In twelve months Nokia may find that very few people can afford the phone and they would have been better developing a more basic model.

Conclusion

Changing demand can cause headaches for business owners. In times of falling sales business owners work hard to try to stop their product being as hard hit as others. Even in times of increasing demand they have difficult decisions to make: should prices be increased or should an investment be made in future growth?

Talking Point

Why might the government be particularly keen to forecast changes in demand?

Revision Essentials

Changing demand – **businesses have to adapt their plans depending on whether demand is increasing or decreasing.**

Economic growth – **the rate at which demand is changing in the economy.**

Exercises

(A and B: 23 marks; 40 minutes)

A1. State how changes in demand affect economic growth. (2)

2. Explain three reasons why there might be a change in the level of demand for Topshop's latest clothing range. (6)

3. Describe two ways in which a small independent clothing business might deal with a significant fall in demand. (4)

B   In 2005, Northern Ireland saw house prices rocket by an average of 22 per cent. In some areas the rise was as high as 60 per cent. Part of the increase in prices has been put down to rise in demand for properties.

1. Explain how increased demand leads to a rise in prices. (2)

2. State three types of business that are likely to benefit from the increase in demand for houses. (3)

3. Eventually, demand fell for houses in Northern Ireland. Describe the likely effect of this on:

   a) estate agents (2)

   b) people who have just purchased a house with a mortgage (2)

   c) first-time buyers? (2)

Classroom Activity

(Groups of 3; 30 minutes)

In 2009 the global economy saw a fall in economic growth. Demand in the UK was falling because consumers had less money to spend each month.

With your classmates, come up with a business idea that may work in a period when the economy is struggling.

Be ready to present your idea to the class, justifying why you think it will be a success.

Practice Questions

Mulberry, founded in 1971, is a British company famous for its luxury leather goods.

The company now has stores throughout the UK, Europe, America and Asia.

In 2009 Mulberry issued a profits warning following falling sales in the ten-week run up to Christmas.

In a statement a spokesperson for Mulberry told a *Times* journalist that the profit warning

was 'a result of the slowdown in consumer demand'. Mulberry was not the only luxury brand to experience problems: famous leather-goods maker Hermes also warned of falling sales.

Adapted from: *The Times*, 11 December 2008

At the same time some companies were fairing much better. Discount chain Poundland saw revenue leap by £50m in one year, with profits over £8m. Chief executive Jim McCarthy said: 'We are the success story of the times. We are getting more and more posh customers. They used to boast how much their houses have gone up in value or how much their cars cost. Now they throw dinner parties to brag how much they've saved on loo rolls.'

Adapted from: *The Express and Star*, 6 April 2009

Questions

(12 marks; 25 minutes)

1 At the time these articles were written, the UK was experiencing a recession. Explain why high end, luxury brands such as Muberry and Hermes might suffer in a recession. (6)

2 Explain two reasons why companies such as Poundland might experience increases in sales and profits during a recession. (6)

Chapter 13

Inflation

$50 billion for an egg? Impossible. Not if they were Zimbabwe dollars. On 18 July 2008 one egg was priced at 50bn Zimbabwean dollars (around 17p).

This crazy situation began in 2006, when the Zimbabwean government announced that it had printed an extra 60 trillion Zimbabwean dollars. It was to pay government officials, soldiers and policemen vastly increased salaries to keep them loyal to the government. The government continued to print more and more money in order to fund projects and pay its staff. With each increase in the amount of money available, businesses realised that bank notes were worth less and less. So they increased their prices – again and again. The $50bn egg was the result.

In Zimbabwe's economy prices (not just of eggs) were rising rapidly. In fact, in 2008 economists calculated that prices were rising by 231 million per cent annually. When the average price of goods rises in an economy there is **inflation.**

A Zimbabwean 50 billion dollar note

Why does inflation happen?

In Zimbabwe inflation occurred because the government printed more and more money. (This is actually very rare, although the UK government did print extra money in 2009 to attempt to reduce the effects of the credit crunch.)

Inflation normally happens for one of two reasons:

- **The cost of resources increases**. When resources become more scarce their value and therefore price increases. Resources may become scarce because they are non-renewable natural resources. The only single resource that can have a significant effect on inflation (price rises generally) is oil.

Oil is the key raw material in a wide range of products, from paint to plastics, and from carpets to clothing. It also, of course, makes petrol, diesel and kerosene (used to fly planes).

- **The demand for resources increases**. Chapter 12 explained that the economy sometimes experiences increases in demand. When businesses see that demand is rising sharply, they are tempted to increase the price, which contributes to inflation. Increases in demand also make resources scarce. As resources become scarcer, their value and price rises.

How is inflation measured?

Economists measure inflation using a standard 'basket of goods'. This basket is representative of what average people spend their money on throughout a year. Researchers find out how much the basket would cost to buy each month. Then they report by how much the total price has increased as a percentage. This figure is reported as the **Consumer Price Index (CPI)**.

What does inflation mean for businesses?

If the costs of a business increase they often pass these price rises on to the consumer. If they identify an increase in demand they will simply add an appropriate amount to the price. For a market trader, it may be as simple as shouting out a different price to passers-by. In other cases it will involve repricing products on the shelves, updating computer systems and reprinting catalogues or menus.

On the other hand, inflation may catch out businesses. A company may be committed to selling a product to a customer at a fixed price for a period of time. If inflation increases their costs they will find their profit margin has been squeezed or, worse, that they are selling at a loss.

Inflation, like economic growth is also hard to predict. Uncertainty is unwelcome for businesses as it prevents them planning ahead.

What does inflation mean for individuals?

When the CPI is 3 per cent it means that the basket of goods is costing 3 per cent more to purchase compared with this time last year. Whenever the CPI is positive you will hear journalists and individuals commenting that the **cost of living** is increasing, meaning that on average it costs more to buy things than it used to.

Conclusion

Inflation is when the general level of prices in an economy increases. Inflation occurs when a business is faced with higher costs or because there is increased demand that is pushing up prices. Inflation is costly for most businesses, as it requires time-consuming adjustments to prices.

> ### Talking Point
>
> If inflation is 3 per cent and average wages are increasing by 3 per cent a year, does inflation really matter?

Revision Essentials

Consumer Price Index – a percentage figure that shows how much prices are increasing per year.

Cost of living – when prices are rising people describe the cost of living as increasing.

Inflation – an increase in the general level of prices in an economy.

Exercises

(A and B: 17 marks; 30 minutes)

A1. Describe in your own words what is meant by the term 'inflation'. (2)

2. For each of the six statements below, state whether they are causes or effects of inflation. (6)

Prices of the raw materials for products are rising, which makes business costs rise	People and businesess feel uncertain	Some people feel worse off if their incomes remain the same
Businesses may need to pay to change their price lists and menus	More people want products and suppliers cannot currently meet the demand	Borrowing is likely to increase

3. Explain why an increasing demand for products can lead to inflation. (3)

B   A survey has revealed that inflation is seriously affecting football supporters. Fans are paying 30 per cent more for tickets, rail travel, merchandise and pay-per-view TV than they did three years ago.

     Adapted from: *The Independent*, 29 July 2009

1. To what extent do you think inflation will affect people who support a football team? (6)

Classroom Activity

(Groups of 2 or 3; 30 minutes)

You have been given the following shopping list by your older sister:

- a fashion magazine
- 1 carton of 100 per cent fresh orange juice
- 1 pack of digestive biscuits
- 4 quilted toilet rolls
- 2 loaves of white thick-sliced bread.

Using the internet, work with your partner to find out how much this will cost.

Now imagine that inflation this year will be 10 per cent. Now calculate how much the shopping would be next year.

Discuss with your partner how inflation may impact on your family.

Practice Questions

The UK has never experienced the same level of inflation as Zimbabwe but has seen a steady rise in prices over time. The table shows the increase in the price of a loaf of bread between 1970 and 2007.

Date	Price of loaf
1970	9p
1980	33p
1990	50p
2000	52p
2007	94p

Questions

(10 marks; 30 minutes)

1 Which of the following is *not* a significant cause of inflation? (1)

   a) increase in demand

   b) more people attending university

   c) increases in business costs.

2 Explain why the price of bread is often used as a way of measuring inflation. (3)

3 Explain the impact of increasing inflation on the following groups: (6)

   a) a family living in the UK

   b) the Government

   c) a local business.

Chapter 14

Unemployment

Every month the Government publishes the number of people who are looking for a job but cannot find one. The number of people **unemployed** is calculated by the Government to be the number of people attending Job Centres seeking work who claim Job Seekers Allowance (JSA). The Government calls this method the **Claimant Count**.

Unemployment and changing demand

Unemployment is typically at its highest when demand in the economy is low. When demand is low, firms are selling less and therefore don't require as many workers to create stocks. As demand in the economy increases, firms hire extra workers to deal with the increases in demand.

Costs of unemployment to the individual

- *Reduction in income*: unemployment will mean the individual may no longer be able to afford to pay for items he or she previously could, such as a mortgage on a house

- *Skill loss*: being out of work for a long period of time may mean that the individual's employment skills are lost, making it harder to find another job.

- *Loss of self-esteem*: society often takes a negative view of the unemployed, which can reduce confidence and increase the chances of depression.

Costs of unemployment to the economy

- *Increase in costs to the government*: unemployed individuals are normally eligible for JSA and housing benefits. These are paid for by the government, which in turn raises its money from taxes on individuals and businesses.

- *Opportunity cost*: the unemployed individual could have been producing goods for the economy and paying income tax to the government

- *Potential increase in crime*: unemployed individuals are more likely to be involved in crime, which will have negative effects on society.

What can be done about unemployment?

In the long term, the best way to reduce unemployment is to stimulate increases in demand so that businesses voluntarily want to hire extra workers. In the short term, the Government can provide extra education and training or offer to pay part of a worker's wages to make unemployed workers more attractive to businesses.

The Science Bit

Be careful when comparing unemployment figures. The UK Government uses the Claimant Count but other institutions use the Labour Force Survey (LFS). The LFS is similar but doesn't require that people claim Job Seekers Allowance, so will also include those who are too embarrassed or ineligible to claim financial support.

Conclusion

The number of people who are unemployed depends on the amount of demand in the economy. Unemployment is damaging to both the individual and society and the government therefore tries to reduce the number of unemployed by offering education and training and by trying to increase demand in the economy.

Talking Point

Unemployment is often not evenly spread across the country. In July 2009 in parts of Birmingham unemployment was over 10 per cent while in many other areas of the country it was below 2 per cent. Why do you think this was?

Revision Essentials

Claimant count – the measure of unemployment used by the UK Government. It counts the number of people claiming Job Seekers Allowance to estimate the number unemployed.

Unemployment – the number of people out of work and actively seeking work.

Exercises

(A and B: 15 marks; 25 minutes)

A1. In your own words, describe the meaning of the term 'unemployment'. (3)

2. Outline how falling unemployment levels would affect:

a. individual workers (2)

b. the Government (2)

c. the local community. (2)

B In April 2006 Peugeot announced the closure of their factory at Ryton, near Coventry in the West Midlands, leading to the loss of 2,300 jobs.

Adapted from: *The Times,* 18 April 2006

1. State and explain three ways in which increasing unemployment could cause the local area and the UK economy to suffer. (6)

Classroom Activity

(Groups of 3; 30 minutes)

By the end of 2008 China's unemployment hit a 30-year high. This particularly affected those who travelled from rural areas to work in factories in the cities. Many of the factories produced products to be sold abroad. However, as global demand fell, more and more workers found that they had no job to travel to.

Source: http://www.businessweek.com/

In groups of three each person should choose one of the following roles:

● adviser to the government
● travelling worker trying to find a job in a factory
● family of travelling worker.

You need to give your answers to the following questions to the group. Remember to think about how the person in your role would feel.

● How does unemployment affect the rural economy?
● What can be done to reduce the impact of unemployment on the rural economy?

Practice Questions

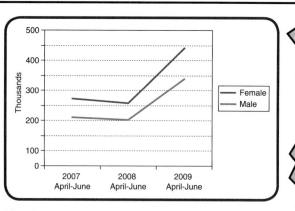

Youth unemployment (18–24) in the UK

Source: National Statistics

Questions

(12 marks; 30 minutes)

1 Which two of the following are true according to the graph? (2)

   a) Employment levels have increased consistently for both men and women between April 2007 and June 2009.
   b) Male unemployment has increased more rapidly than female unemployment between April 2008 and June 2009.
   c) There are less unemployed in May 2009 than May 2007.
   d) Employment levels have fallen between April 2008 and April 2009.

2 One significant factor affecting the UK is the rise in unemployment of 18–24 year olds (often referred to as 'Youth Unemployment'). Suggest two problems the UK economy will face from having higher numbers of 18–24 year olds in unemployment. (4)

3 Anthony McClaran is the chief executive of UCAS, which runs the applications process for universities in the UK. In a 2009 interview with *The Sunday Telegraph* he stated that for the first time applications for university exceeded 600,000.

   Source: *The Daily Telegraph*, 20 August 2009

   To what extent is there a link between the unemployment data and record numbers of people applying to go to University? (6)

Chapter 15

Shocks!

In June 2008 a gas pipeline burst causing a subsequent explosion in Western Australia. The state lost 35 per cent of its energy supply overnight. The mining and manufacturing industries that form a large part of Western Australia's economy require a continuous supply of energy. The sudden loss of energy meant that workers had to be laid off and energy had to be urgently sourced from elsewhere. Even hospital operations were postponed in an attempt to save energy in government buildings. Economists have calculated that it cost Western Australia's economy $6.8bn.

All economies are vulnerable to unexpected external **shocks** that affect the availability and price of resources.

We will shock you?

By their very nature, shocks are unpredictable and unforeseen. There are, however, certain types of shock that do occur quite frequently:

- Changes in global commodity prices such as copper and oil. Prices can rise or fall quickly depending on changes in demand or if it turns out there is more or less remaining than originally thought.
- Natural disasters such as earthquakes can cut production, leading to price increases due to shortages.
- Damage to crops caused by bad weather or disease can cause a shortage of supply that leads to a dramatic increase in price.

- Economic shocks, such as the credit crunch that hit economies between 2007 and 2009, can lead to uncertainty and reduced demand in several major economies.
- The publication of research that a certain type of food, diet or exercise is particularly good or bad for your health can also shock the market for that product.

The impact of shocks

How severely a shock affects an economy is dependent on several factors:

- the availability of alternative resources. If resources can be substituted the impact of the shock will be smaller
- how many people and businesses are dependent on the resource
- the time taken for people and businesses to adjust to the shock.

The UK is blessed with relatively few natural disasters, such as earthquakes, droughts, wars (on home soil) and tsunamis. There have been man-made shocks, though, from sources such as terrorist attacks or bankers' incompetence.

Businesses are frequently accused of exploiting the opportunities that a shock may present. When large parts of England flooded in the summer of 2007 and hundreds of people were unable to travel home, several hotels put their prices up. An economist may respond that they were only responding to changing demand. Stranded travellers presumably felt exploited as hotels took advantage of their unpleasant situation.

Conclusion

No economy is able to escape from the reality that shocks will occur and change the availability and price of resources. The size of the impact depends on availability of substitutes, dependence on the resource, and time taken to adjust to the shock.

Talking Point

Does trading with other countries make an economy more or less vulnerable to a shock?

Revision Essentials

Shock – an unexpected event that affects the economy in terms of availability and price of resources or products.

Exercises

(A and B: 18 marks; 25 minutes)

A1. In your own words explain the term 'economic shock'. (2)

2. Describe one economic shock you are aware of and what impact it had on an economy. (3)

3. Explain why economic shocks can have major consequences for businesses. (5)

B In a BBC Panorama report in 2008 Jeremy Vine reported that in some areas people had seen property prices fall by up to 60 per cent. This was a huge shock, not only to individuals but also to the economy as a whole.

1. State two types of business that will be affected by the fall in house prices. (2)

2. Analyse the impact of the fall in house prices on:

- individuals who currently own their own home (2)
- individuals looking to buy their first house (2)
- house-building companies. (2)

Classroom Activity

(Groups of 4; 40 minutes)

In your team you need to do two things:

- Select an industry area in which you would like to run your own business. Briefly describe your business e.g. 'We have chosen to run a florist. We will rent our building and have three full time staff.'
- Write down on individual sticky notes or cards four examples of economic shocks that could affect a variety of businesses.

Your teacher will collect in all the teams' examples of economic shocks and read them out in turn. You will then discuss the impact that the shock might have on your business.

Practice Questions

Impact of rising food prices

The World Bank approved a US$7m grant to Nicaragua to help the country manage with increasing food prices. The bank aimed to provide immediate relief to the most vulnerable groups and expand the supply of agricultural products. The grant was to be funded through the Food Price Crisis Response Trust Fund launched by the World Bank in May 2008.

The operation focused on two areas:

- ensuring that poor children in the most vulnerable areas continue to receive lunch at school
- supporting small farmers to increase their production.

Adapted from: The World Bank
www.worldbank.org

Questions

(14 marks; 30 minutes)

1 State the meaning of the term 'commodity'. (2)

2 Which one of the following is *not* a commodity product? (2)

   a) rice

   b) sugar

   c) chocolate

   d) copper.

3 Explain why poor people in Nicaragua are more affected by high food prices than those who are more wealthy (4)

4 Explain how the support given to local farmers will have an impact on food prices. (6)

Chapter 16

Exchange rates

In the run-up to Christmas in 2007, airlines flying to New York became particularly busy because hundreds of extra Brits were traveling to the 'Big Apple' to do their Christmas shopping. The reason was that the **exchange rate** had changed. People were able buy all their Christmas presents (clothes, perfume, jewellery, etc.) *and* pay for the return flight for less than the cost of the presents at home. The two days in New York was a bit of a bonus too!

Currencies

The **currency** in America is the US Dollar. Most countries in Europe use the Euro and in Japan they have the Yen. The UK has the Pound. There are over 25 major currencies worldwide.

The value of one unit of currency isn't the same as in another: one dollar may buy you a can of cola in America but one Yen coins aren't even accepted in most vending machines in Japan. What is more, the values between two currencies vary so that one currency can become more valuable in terms of another. The **exchange rate** shows us how much one currency is worth in terms of another.

The case of Christmas shopping in America

Christmas shoppers going to New York from the UK need to exchange their pounds for US dollars.

● In January 2002 £1 could have been exchanged for $1.43.

● By November in 2007 the same £1 could have been swapped for $2.12.

In the graph below, whenever the line goes upwards, it indicates that a pound buys more dollars. Therefore the pound is getting stronger against the dollar. New York shoppers in December 2007 would have felt smug when, a month later, the pound started to fall back against the dollar.

The following Christmas, £1 only bought around $1.50. So every £100 in New York bought $150 of presents. A year before £100 had provided $212 of spending power!

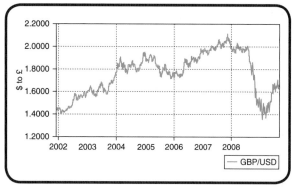

Exchange rate history
Source: http://www.dollars2pounds.com

If travellers had £500, their spending power at different points in time was as shown in Box 1.

	Spending money in £	...gives you spending money in $
January 2001	500	715
November 2007	500	1060
June 2008	500	675
November 2009	500	800

Box 1

The information in Box 1 shows how quickly and how dramatically exchange rates can change over time.

What does the exchange rate mean for businesses?

The impact of the exchange rate depends on what interaction you have with businesses and customers in other countries:

- If you run a business where no materials are sourced from abroad and all your customers are in the same country, the exchange rate matters very little.

- If you import your raw materials from abroad then the exchange rate is very important. If the pound falls in value, imported goods become more expensive for manufacturers and for retailers. For example, if imported bananas become more expensive because of the exchange rate, Innocent Smoothies will make less profit unless they increase their prices (which would hit their sales). Meanwhile, a rising pound – making imports cheaper – would allow Innocent to pass the savings on to the customer or keep the money in the business for investment.

- If you export your product to international customers the exchange rate is important too. A high pound makes UK exports more expensive, forcing an exporter to choose between two unpleasant options:

  - either lose business as people buy less of your higher-priced products

  - or, lose profit by keeping your overseas prices the same (but receiving less in pounds for each export sold).

- If the exchange rate works in your favour you may find customers from abroad switch to you because your prices appear cheaper (such as department stores in New York).

The Science Bit

The value of the pound changes depending on two main factors:

- demand for pounds (how much people want to buy), and
- supply of pounds (how many pounds people want to sell/get rid of).

For example, if the Bank of England increased UK interest rates, foreign savers would buy pounds in order to keep their savings in UK banks earning high interest rates. This increases the price of the pound.

Conclusion

The impact on a business of a change in the exchange rate depends on how exposed it is to the international economy. A corner shop may think it has nothing to do with imports and exports, but perhaps half of all the goods it sells have come from abroad. So, a fall in the pound will push up its costs, forcing it to think about price rises on the shelf. Most businesses have some exposure to exchange rates, whether they realise it or not.

Talking Point

What action would you take if your products appear more expensive to customers in other countries because of the exchange rate?

Revision Essentials

Currency – the unit of money in a particular country or region.

Exchange rate – the price of one currency in terms of another.

Exercises

(A and B: 14 marks; 30 minutes)

A1. What is meant by the term 'exchange rate'? (2)

2. Assume that £1 = €1.25. A Spanish tourist buys three pairs of jeans in London for £30 each. How much in total would they have spent in Euros? (2)

3. If the exchange rate changed to £1 = €1.60 would the Spanish tourist be better or worse off if he bought the jeans? Explain your reasons. (2)

B The table shows the exchange rate of the pound against the US dollar from January 1979 to January 2007. For example, in January 1993 £1 was approximately equal to $1.5.

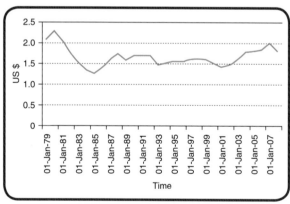

Change in exchange rate over time

Source: The Bank of England

1. State the year in which the £ was weakest against the US$? (1)

2. Which year would have been the best year to travel to New York for a shopping trip, in terms of what you could have bought with your money?. Explain your answer. (3)

3. If a business imports products from the US to sell in the UK, explain how the changes in the exchange rate from 1980 to 1985 may have impacted on their profits. (4)

Classroom Activity

(Groups of 2–3; 40 minutes)

Use the internet to find out the exchange rate for the British pound against the Euro between 1990 and 2009, and plot this information on a graph.

In your groups discuss how the following businesses would be affected as the exchange rate changes:

- a business that provides holidays to Europe
- a company based in Berlin that imports products from the UK.

Practice Questions

After the UK had experienced a significant period of cheap imports from abroad, the pound dramatically weakened against the US dollar during 2008. The effect of this change is that importing products from the US, as well as countries that commonly deal in dollars such as China, has become more expensive.

Approximately 54 per cent of the products in the Argos catalogue are made in China and this has been the main contributor to the 5 per cent increase, on average, of prices in the catalogue.

An article in The Guardian quoted accountants PricewaterhouseCoopers who warned that rising import costs would cost British shoppers £10bn. Argos reacted to this by introducing more value lines.

Adapted from *The Guardian*, 19 July 2009

Questions

(14 marks; 30 minutes)

1. Which of the following is an effect of the pound becoming weaker against the US$? (1)
    a) Businesses who export products to the US may see an increase in orders.
    b) It is cheaper for British tourists when they are in America.
    c) Importing goods from abroad becomes cheaper.
2. Describe how a falling exchange rate affects a business that relies heavily on importing products. (3)
3. Explain how British consumers might react to the 5 per cent increase in prices at Argos. (4)
4. Prices at Argos are published in its catalogue twice a year. Explain how Argos might be affected more by changes in exchange rates than Amazon.com, a purely online business. (6)

Chapter 17

Interest rates

In March 2009 the **Bank of England** set **interest rates** at an all-time low of 0.5 per cent. This was to encourage people to spend more money in the economy, to avoid entering a deeper economic recession. By making it cheaper to borrow money (and less beneficial to save it) consumers and businesses would be more likely to spend and thereby increase economic activity.

The interest rate is the yearly fee for borrowing money and the reward for saving it. If the interest rate is 10 per cent then the borrower of £100 must pay back £110 at the end of a year.

Savers, meanwhile, are paid interest on any money they deposit in the bank. If you had £100 in the bank and the interest rate was 5 per cent the bank would pay you £5 interest at the end of the year.

Table 1 shows the effects on borrowing and saving of changing the interest rate.

Table 1

Interest rate (%)	Likely to borrow?	Likely to save?	Expected impact on economic activity
Up	Less	More	Down
Down	More	Less	Up

The effect of lower interest rates

Lower interest rates make existing and future borrowing cheaper, increasing the likelihood of extra spending. Savers find that saving is no longer fruitful and are tempted to spend rather than continue to save.

In 2009 those with variable mortgages saw their repayments fall drastically. Amarjit Singh saw his repayments fall by £721 a month as a result of the Bank of England's action to cut interest rates from 4.5% to 0.5% (Source: *Daily Telegraph,* 6 March 2009.)

Amarjit (and thousands like him) will have then been able to spend more on products he and his family would otherwise not have been able to afford.

The effect of higher interest rates

Higher interest rates will put people off borrowing more money by using credit cards and personal loans. They may be tempted to save more money, as the rewards for doing so are greater. This reduces the amount of money they are willing and able to spend on goods and services. Most businesses will be affected badly by this, especially those selling non-essential goods such as expensive perfume and luxury holidays.

The increase will also make investment in new machinery more expensive for businesses so they will be less likely to do so. So sales can slump for firms, such as the producers of forklift trucks.

Interest rates and the economic cycle

The Bank of England changes the interest rate in an attempt to control economic activity and prevent inflation and unemployment.

It will increase the interest rate when it fears that the economy is growing too quickly and suffering from the effects of inflation. It will cut the interest rate if it wants to expand the economy and reduce unemployment.

The graph below shows the relationship between economic growth and the interest rate. Other variables influence the relationship but it shows that when the interest rate is increased, economic growth falls and vice versa.

Comparison of economic growth and interest rate
Source: Figures from www.measuringworth.org

The Science Bit

In Chapter 4 you saw how products and services are in greater demand when the price is lower. This same principle is at work here: by reducing the interest rate the Bank of England is effectively reducing the price of money and therefore increasing demand for borrowing it.

Conclusion

Businesses and the economy as a whole are affected dramatically by changes in the interest rate. Those companies selling luxuries benefit from a reduction in the interest rate, while those selling budget basics often benefit in times of an increase. Similarly, businesses are more likely to risk expansion in times of lower interest rates. When rates go up, they are more likely to focus on survival.

Talking Point

Who are the most important stakeholders in the Bank of England's decision to change the interest rate?

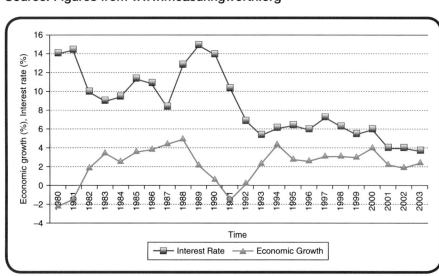

Revision Essentials

Bank of England – the institution responsible for setting the interest rate on a monthly basis.

Interest rate – the percentage that shows how expensive it is to borrow money and how beneficial it is to save it.

Exercises

(14 marks; 20 minutes)

1. Define 'interest rate' in your own words. (2)

2. Why might someone who took a variable rate mortgage in 2009 be unhappy with a 2 per cent increase in the Bank of England's base rate? (3)

3. Explain the effect of a fall in interest rates on:

   - Wolseley plc (the world's largest distributer of plumbing and building materials) (3)
   - a small designer clothing shop, due to open next month (3)
   - a retired couple with £50,000 of savings. (3)

Classroom Activity

(This should take about 20 minutes, with groups of up to 6. At the end group is could feed back to the class about some of the effects that they noted.)

Five group members should work together to each choose a stakeholder of a large manufacturing company they are familiar with. They should each write their stakeholder on a sticky note and briefly describe their relationship with the company. They should attach this sticky note to them, or the table in front of them.

The final group member is the Governor of the Bank of England. Starting with the current interest rate he or she should write three new rates (moving up or down) on separate pieces of card.

The Governor should then turn over the cards, one at a time in front of him or her on the table. Starting with the current base rate, as a card is turned, each member of the team should describe and explain the impact that this interest rate change will have on them.

Practice Questions

UK interest rates lowered to 0.5%

On 5 March 2009 the Bank of England announced it was cutting interest rates to 0.5 per cent, an all-time low. This was the sixth rate cut since October 2008 and was a direct response to lower consumer spending and a fall in business investment. Together this resulted in a sharp drop in demand in the final quarter of 2008. Unemployment had risen and the market conditions remained difficult.

The Governor of the Bank of England, Mervyn King, said the policy would 'eventually work'.

'Nothing in life is ever certain, but these measures we think will work in the long-term', he said.

Source: The Bank of England

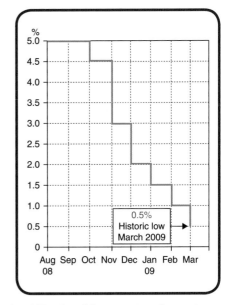

Bank of England base rates August 2008–March 2009

Questions

(16 marks; 20 minutes)

1 What effects would the Bank of England expect following a cut in interest rates? Select two answers from below. (2)

   a) Businesses who have loans will need to pay back more money to their banks.

   b) Individuals who have savings will gain a greater return.

   c) People will be more likely to spend money.

   d) The price of oil will rise.

   e) Businesses would be more willing to invest in new machinery.

2 Explain why the Bank of England believed that cutting the interest rate would help increase consumer spending. (3)

3 Explain how reducing the interest rate may help to reduce unemployment in the UK. (3)

4 In your opinion, which is the better way to get consumers and businesses to spend more – reducing interest rates or cutting taxes? Justify your answer. (8)

Chapter 18

Government spending and taxation

When a famous Liverpool footballer misplaced his payslip showing how much he earned in October 2007, it was published in several newspapers. Readers were amazed. The story was not how much the footballer got paid (whopping footballers' wages had been in the news for several years). Instead the focus was on how much tax he paid to the government. In one month, the footballer paid enough tax to pay three teachers' yearly salaries.

Why does the government collect and spend money?

The Government has a duty to provide basic services such as health care and housing to those who cannot afford it themselves. The Government also provides services that no profit-driven businesses would be willing to provide for *everyone*. These include: defence (the Army, Navy and Air Force), the police, schools and maintaining roads.

Where does the money go?

The Chancellor of the Exchequer had a £517.7bn budget in 2007–08 for England. (Just for reference, £1bn is the equivalent 24 million record National Lottery jackpots!)

- £90.7bn was spent on the National Health Service.

- £41.2bn was spent in schools.

- £125.3bn was spent on benefits such as pensions, Job Seekers Allowance and income support.

- £6.7bn was spent on policing.

- £5.3bn was spent on international aid.

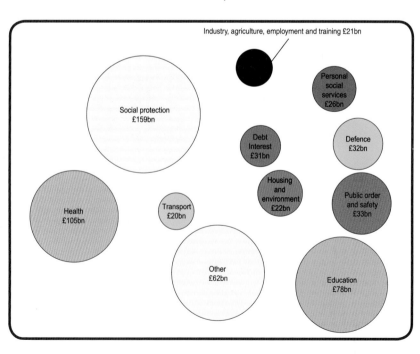

Government Spending 2007–08

Where does the money come from?

The Government's spending is paid for through the collection of taxes. The Government has three main sources of taxes:

1. *Taxes on income.* People in work pay a percentage of their income direct to the Government. Generally speaking, people who earn more pay more income tax.

2. *Taxes on purchases.* Value added tax (VAT) is a percentage of the selling price added on to most goods purchased in an economy. Specific items such as alcohol, cigarettes, petrol and houses have their own specific sales taxes at various rates.

3. *Taxes on company profits.* The Government takes a percentage of the profits made by every company at the end of each tax year. This is called corporation tax.

When the economy is doing well, tax income is high because individuals are earning and spending, and businesses are making big profits. **Government spending** is also low, as fewer people need benefits to support their income.

In recessions, the opposite is the case: the tax revenues fall but spending must increase to support the population, e.g. the unemployed.

The Government often doesn't have enough money to meet its objectives so it borrows money, just like individuals and businesses do. In July 2009 alone it borrowed £9bn and in 2007–08 as a whole spent £29.9bn on interest on its debts!

Can the taxation and spending solve society's problem?

The Government attempts to make some goods and services less attractive to society by putting large taxes on them. Activities that have large negative externalities such as smoking, drinking and motoring are often highly taxed. The higher taxes on petrol and owning a car make it more expensive to drive, with the aim of reducing pollution and congestion.

The Government can also make certain things more attractive by reducing taxes or even providing subsidies. Tax on fresh food is lower than it is on sweets or biscuits. Businesses providing jobs in areas with high unemployment may receive discounts on their tax bills.

Spending is often focused on vulnerable areas of society such as the disabled or those on no or low incomes. For example, those on low incomes may be tempted to turn to crime if the government did not support them whilst each year the elderly receive a 'Winter Fuel Payment' to help them heat their homes.

However, the Government often struggles to solve problems effectively. People on high incomes often complain they see little personal benefit for the large amounts of tax they pay. In fact, many employ accountants to exploit loopholes to reduce their tax bills. They often pay little more in tax than people with far lower incomes.

It can be claimed that high taxes on alcohol, cigarettes and petrol have done little to reduce binge drinking, smoking and driving. If people are addicted to smoking, how much will the price have to rise before people give up?

The Science Bit

In the UK, income tax is charged at different rates depending on how much you earn. In 2009, most people had a tax-free allowance up to £6,035 and then paid 20 per cent on every pound they earned up to £34,800. Then, for every pound they earned above £34,800 they paid 40 per cent in tax. Russia, Iceland and several other Eastern European countries have a 'flat' tax system where everyone pays the same percentage, no matter how much they earn.

Conclusion

Governments take a share of income, spending and profits to support vulnerable people in society and provide non-profit-making services. Governments must decide how much to get involved in society. Should they take a lot of tax and spend heavily on vulnerable people or should they take a little and focus only on the exceptionally needy? The answer often depends on your view of just what 'needy' means.

Talking Point

Consider the 'Science Bit' box. Would you like to see your country move towards a flat tax system? Can you think of any other alternatives?

Revision Essentials

Government spending – **money spent by the Government to provide essential services that profit-driven businesses would not.**

Taxation – **money raised by the Government from taking a share of income, spending and profits.**

Exercises

(A and B: 17 marks; 35 minutes)

A1. State the three areas where the Government spends most of its budget. (3)

2. The chart below shows the changes in UK Government spending over 20 years.

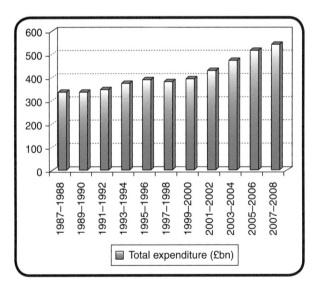

Government Spending
Source: Financial Times, 22 June 2009

Between which years did the UK Government increase spending most rapidly? (2)

3. Spending on health in 1997–98 was just under £40bn and by 2007–08 had risen to just under £100bn. Give two possible reasons why the Government chose to spend so much more on health care. (4)

B In 2008, VAT in the UK was reduced from 17.5 per cent to 15 per cent. This meant that an item priced at £39.99 would now be £39.14. UK businesses were given a deadline of December 2008 to prepare for the reduction. In January 2010 the VAT was put back up to 17.5 per cent.

Retailers broadly welcomed the scheme but were concerned about the short deadline in order to get ready.

1. State two stakeholders who should benefit from the tax cut. (2)

2. Describe the impact of the tax cut on consumers. (3)

3. Explain why retailers might be concerned about the short deadline given to adapt to the new tax rate. (3)

Classroom Activity

(Groups of 3–4; 30 minutes)

Imagine you have been given £1bn to use in your local area. You have the following areas in which you can spend the money:

- education
- health
- public order (e.g. police)
- housing and community
- recreation, culture and religion (e.g. parks, museums)
- environmental protection.

In your teams discuss how you would you decide to spend the money and what you would be spending it on.

Do you think that you could solve all the problems in your local area with money? Be ready to give your feedback to the class.

Practice Questions

It is estimated that the social costs of binge-drinking in the UK are over £20bn annually.

This includes costs paid for National Health Service and the police. The Government has a number of measures that it could look at to try to reduce the levels of binge-drinking. These include: increasing the price of alcohol; limiting opening times of pubs, bars and clubs; and running advertising campaigns highlighting the dangers of binge-drinking.

Questions

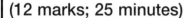

(12 marks; 25 minutes)

1 If local councils were given the power to increase the price of alcohol, what impact do you think there would be on the quantity of alcohol demanded? (4)

2 To what extent do you think that taxation or government spending would be successful in reducing the numbers of people binge-drinking in the UK? (8)

BIG OR SMALL?

Chapter 19

Internal and external business growth

When Bill Gates set up Microsoft in 1975, it was hard to imagine how much the business would grow. Microsoft's growth has been due to its ability to spot an opportunity and exploit it. Microsoft was making operating-system software and by 1986 the company was valued at just over $1bn. As Microsoft entered into the games-consoles and portable-music market with the Xbox and Zune, the company grew to a 2009 valuation of over $75bn. Microsoft has grown by constantly improving what they do for their customers.

In contrast, LOVEFiLM has used loans to incorporate *ten* rival businesses (and their members) into their organisation, allowing them to grow quickly. In the space of seven years this has earned them 1.25 million subscribers and made them the third largest business of its type in the UK.

How do you measure business size?

Comparing the size of businesses can be difficult because people have different ways to measure business size. Below are the main methods that are used:

- *The value of the business.* This means how much it would cost to purchase the business from its owners.

- *Market share.* This refers to the number of customers the business has as a percentage of the whole market.

- *How much revenue the business has.* This measures the £s value of all the sales the business makes in a year.

- *The amount of profit the business has made.* For example, in the first half of 2009 Ted Baker plc made £6 million profit. In the same period, the much larger Next plc made £199 million profit.

- *The value of the assets owned by the business.* Assets include buildings, machinery, equipment and cash. Their value can be added together to calculate business size.

If any of these methods show an increase in business size there is **business growth.** It is important to be cautious, however, when using one method in isolation. It is perfectly possible for a firm to grow using one method while also appearing to shrink if using another method. For this reason it is best to compare business size using more than one method.

Types of business growth

Internal growth means that the business growth is achieved as a result of its own actions or decisions; no other businesses are involved. **External growth** is an increase in business size as a result of purchasing one business and incorporating it into another (known as a **takeover**), or when two businesses agree to join together (known as a **merger**).

Internal growth

Growing internally normally involves making the business more appealing to more customers.

- Improving the marketing mix will either make the existing customers purchase products more frequently (or for a higher price) or tempt new customers to buy for the first time. This will lead to increased revenue and probably increased profit and market share – and therefore business growth.

- Innovation and research and development could also lead to the business developing new products where it can immediately take a major share of the sales. For example, Sky continues to create new products such as Sky+ and Sky+HD. This leads to more customers signing up to Sky's subscription service which leads to an increased business size.

Internal growth is normally financed by reinvesting profits made in previous years. For this reason, internal growth can be quite slow, and requires that profits have actually been made in the past.

External growth

External growth is when the size of a business is increased because it has joined forces with another business, either through a takeover or a merger. Whereas internal growth is slow and steady, external growth is sudden. If Tesco bought the French supermarket giant Carrefour, Tesco would double in size overnight. Joining two businesses means an immediate leap in revenues, profits, market share and assets.

Purchasing another business usually requires a large amount of money, for example the £10,000m that Kraft offered to buy Cadbury in 2009. Usually, the only businesses that can afford such huge sums have already had a period of success or can persuade banks that their strategy for growth is very likely to succeed.

Unfortunately most takeovers do not succeed. Research shows that the majority leave the combined businesses in a worse shape than they were before! This is because bringing two companies (and their workforces) together is frequently troublesome. Managers underestimate the difficulties caused and overestimate their ability to handle them. When two businesses merge there is often only one set of staff needed for each job function, so staff spend longer on fighting for their jobs than serving the customers.

Conclusion

Small businesses normally increase in size through internal growth. They will seek to improve their marketing mix and be innovative in an attempt to take sales and market share from rivals. They may even identify a new market to enjoy all for themselves until competitors arrive.

Larger businesses have more choice in their strategy for growth. They may choose to grow steadily internally as this impacts little on staff and means that they can maintain much more control over the culture of business. However, they may try to grow quickly at the risk of disagreements and loss of control.

Talking Point

Why might shareholders prefer external growth while other stakeholders prefer internal growth?

Revision Essentials

External growth – an increase in business size as a result of a merger or takeover.

Internal growth – an increase in business size as a result of the business's own actions or decisions.

Merger – where two businesses agree to join forces and begin trading as one.

Takeover – where one business purchases another and incorporates it into its own operation.

Exercises

(A and B: 26 marks; 40 minutes)

A1. Describe two ways in which a business can increase in size through internal growth. (4)

2. Define the terms:

   a) merger

   b) takeover. (4)

3. Suggest three ways in which you could measure business growth. (3)

4. Which of the following is an example of external growth?

   a) Lisa's clothes store now stocks a kids range.

   b) a vacuum cleaner business has invested in new research and development.

   c) a large multinational has taken over an ice-cream business. (2)

B Teresa has been a hairdresser for over 20 years; after working in salons she worked from home as a mobile hairdresser. However, she missed the buzz of working in a salon and decided to set up her own business, Strands. She started in small premises on the outskirts of Worcester city centre but recently moved to a new larger building in town. She has increased the number of staff who work for her and she now has a beauty salon and nail bar running in the same building.

1. Explain which element of the marketing mix Teresa has changed in the process of expanding her business. (3)

2. Describe two ways in which the expansion of Teresa's business might benefit her customers. (4)

3. Explain the impact Teresa's expansion may have had on two other stakeholder groups. (6)

Classroom Activity

(Groups of 3–4; 30 minutes)

Your teacher will give you a business name that you are familiar with. You have 30 minutes to put a plan together of how you might like to expand the business; you can choose if you would like to do this internally or externally.

Practice Questions

Innocent Drinks has experienced rapid internal growth since its launch in 1999.

In April 2009 Richard Reed, Co-founder of Innocent Drinks, announced a £30m deal with Coca-Cola. Coca-Cola is believed to have purchased a stake of between 10–20 per cent in the company that has experienced rapid internal growth since its launch in 1999.

In a recent interview Mr Reed explained that the partnership would first allow Innocent to expand further into Europe and then across the globe and would help a business which, this year, made a loss and needed to make some staff redundant.

However, despite enthusiasm from the founders this growth plan has been criticised by other stakeholders. Some customers believe Innocent has 'sold out' a brand that stood for being socially and environmentally aware. They believe it should not have accepted cash from one of the biggest American multinational businesses.

In their press release, however, the founders explain:

'They (Coca-Cola) have a small stake of between 10–20 per cent, which they paid £30m for. We chose Coca-Cola as our minority investor because as well as providing the funds, they can help us get our products out to more people in more places. Plus, they have been in business for over 120 years, so there will be things we can learn from them. And in some small ways we may be able to influence their thinking too.'

Source: www.innocentdrinks.co.uk

Questions

(15 marks; 25 minutes)

1 Describe two reasons for the partnership between Coca-Cola and Innocent Drinks. (4)

2 To what extent may the image of Innocent have changed in the eyes of different stakeholders following this news? (6)

3 Do you think Innocent's founders were right to accept Coca-Cola's investment? Explain your view. (5)

Chapter 20

The benefits and drawbacks of business growth

Sarah Tremellen started Bravissimo in 1994. Bravissimo specialises in underwear and swimwear for larger women. The company grew by 300 per cent in its first year and 200 per cent in its second, with 70 per cent growth each year since. This growth has given Bravissimo some huge benefits but has also given some real headaches, which the business has had to work hard to overcome. For example, the business has been able to afford further expansion into twenty high street locations and create a website that brings in around 10 per cent of all the business's sales. However, Sarah has found it hard to keep a large number of staff motivated and there have been difficulties in moving premises and managing finance.

Benefits of growth

The benefits of growth are known as **economies of scale** and happen as businesses become larger. Below are three examples:

- When ordering from suppliers big businesses often expect (and get) a discount for placing large orders. As firms grow (and their orders get bigger) they gain market power. As a result, their suppliers become more dependent on their custom and offer them larger discounts. These discounts can then be passed on to customers, increasing the possibility of further growth as a result of increased competitiveness. The discounts are known as 'bulk-buying' and were the subject of media attention in 2008–09, when Tesco and Walmart were accused of exploiting their size by putting unfair pressure on suppliers to sell at ever lower prices.

- Larger businesses are more likely to be able to secure the high-level investment required to invest in expensive equipment. They can also afford to fund innovation that will make them more efficient or more competitive. New technology is often expensive but can create savings or give competitive advantage over a period of time, which will lead to further growth.

- When firms are small then more one member of staff may fulfil several roles. For example, someone may do the accounts and look after the advertising. They will be reasonably good at both jobs. However, when a business grows it has the potential to hire an expert in accounts and an expert in advertising, making the business more effective and efficient. This benefit is known as **specialisation.**

Drawbacks of growth

The drawbacks of growth are known as **diseconomies of scale** and happen as businesses become larger.

In the early years of a business good entrepreneurs are able to inspire and motivate a small team. They will make each person feel part of the success of the business and motivate him or her to help the business succeed. However, as firms grow they will take on more staff and inevitably some are further away from the top than they would like to be.

The leaders of the business will then begin to find communication more difficult as messages are passed through layers of managers. The result is that it becomes a struggle to respond quickly to changes, to motivate everyone and to have everyone pulling in the same direction. Slow decision-making, discontented staff, falling productivity and worsening customer service are big indicators of diseconomies of scale.

Rate of growth and diseconomies of scale

Some diseconomies of scale can be avoided if the business plans its growth carefully. This will include:

- planning the recruitment and training of new workers in advance so that the process can be done carefully to ensure staff are suitable and trained for the position they will be in

- investing in technology to make communication quick and efficient

- having a flexible structure that means the business can respond quickly to change.

However, careful planning of growth is not always possible, particularly when slow growth may result in a missed opportunity to exploit a gap in the market.

The Science Bit

Economists often draw a diagram to illustrate the benefits and drawbacks of growth.

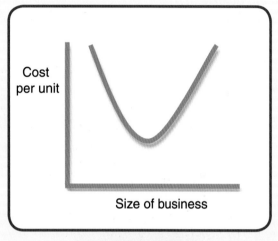

Drawbacks of growth

As the business grows the cost of producing each single unit falls initially as the firm benefits more and more from economies of scale. However, eventually cost per unit begins to rise again as the firm falls victim to diseconomies of scale.

Conclusion

As businesses grow, they tend to benefit from economies of scale and enjoy the benefits of being bigger. However, with growth also comes a drawback known as diseconomies of scale. The point at which the drawbacks begin to outweigh the benefits is dependent on the business and the leadership style of the management, as well as the rate of growth. A manufacturing business employing few staff will continue to benefit from more production because it can afford even more efficient machinery. A florist who struggles to train and trust her staff will notice the difficulties of dealing with all the hand-made orders herself rather more quickly.

Talking Point

To what extent do you agree that the drawbacks of growth are due to growing too quickly.

Revision Essentials

Economies of scale – when a business benefits from its growth.

Diseconomies of scale – when a business suffers as a result of business growth.

Specialisation – focusing on one job role, making it easier to become steadily more expert.

Exercises

(A and B: 15 marks; 30 minutes)

A1. Explain what is meant by the term 'economies of scale'? (2)

2. Describe two benefits of growth to a business. (4)

3. Explain how growth might lead to breakdowns in communication between staff in a business. (3)

B   With almost 30 per cent market share, Tesco has high levels of power over its suppliers. This gives Tesco increased control over the prices it pays and has led to some negative press as it squeezes down the prices it pays to suppliers.

To what extent does size allow Tesco to benefit from lower costs from suppliers? (6)

Classroom Activity

(Groups of 6; 30 minutes)

In your group choose one of the following stakeholder groups:

- pupils
- parents
- governors
- local residents
- local authority
- staff.

Imagine that your school is exploring the idea of merging with another local school. Imagining you are in the role you selected from the list above, consider how this particular stakeholder would feel and make notes for a group discussion.

At the end of the discussion you will need to summarise your group's points and feedback.

Practice Questions

The Davis Service Group is a leading British-based provider of textile maintenance services. This includes: linen hire, rental of work-wear and laundry/washroom services. The Group's revenue is over £950m a year.

The Davis Service Group consists of a number of different businesses focusing on different markets and in 2001 had three main areas:

- textile maintenance (through a company called 'Sunlight')
- providing temporary building systems
- tool hire.

At this time all these businesses operated only in the UK and the Davis Service Group wanted to expand overseas. The managers decided to focus on the textile maintenance division and in 2002 The Davis Service Group took over Berendsen. Berendsen was a very similar business to Sunlight but based in a number of European countries. At the time, Berendsen was not as profitable as Sunlight.

Adapted from: *The Times 100*, www.thetimes100.co.uk

Questions

(17 marks; 30 minutes)

1 State whether the takeover of Berendsen represents internal or external growth. Explain your answer. (3)

2 Explain how three stakeholders would be affected by this takeover. (6)

3 Evaluate the choice by The Davis Service Group to take over Berendsen rather than expand Sunlight overseas. (8)

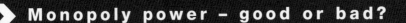
Chapter 21

The benefits and drawbacks of monopoly

Following a court decision, in 2008 the European Union handed Microsoft a €899m fine. Microsoft was accused of using its monopoly position on Windows software to prevent competitors from developing rival software products.

What is a monopoly?

A business is considered to be in a monopoly position when it has some degree of control over the market in which it operates. If there are no rivals in the market a monopolist can charge a greedily high price. If the product or service is a necessity such as energy or water, it could charge virtually any price, and customers would just have to find the money to pay for it. A monopolist can also supply sub-standard quality and service because there is no fear that customers can switch to a competitor.

The key is the strength of the competition. The absence of credible competition means monopolists are free to act as they please. For this reason monopolists are often tempted to put barriers in the way of would-be rivals who aim to compete against them. If a new company dares to enter the market, a monopolist might cut prices until the newcomer goes out of business – before returning prices back to 'normal' levels.

Monopolies and stakeholders

Charging high prices for products or services and/ or continually providing poor-quality service is obviously damaging to customers.

BAA Airports have been owners of the three main airports in London. They were accused of inferior services for passengers and airlines until the Government became involved. In 2009 BAA was forced by the government to sell off Gatwick Airport. Immediately the new owners announced plans to cut queues in order to try to win business from Heathrow.

Businesses with market power often put the squeeze on their suppliers. When Tesco realised that their custom was the only thing keeping several producers going it was able to demand far lower prices. Some farmers claimed that these low prices then pushed them to the edge of bankruptcy.

Monopolists are often slow to respond to changes in the market. Why would a monopolist in the provision of broadband invest in faster connections when customers have nowhere else to go?

Meanwhile, shareholders of businesses behaving this way are unlikely to want to put a stop to it because it means higher profits for them to share.

Is it all bad?

However, just because a business is in a monopoly situation doesn't mean that it automatically charges high prices for inferior products. The most obvious reason for this is that governments have put things in place to prevent this situation happening (see Chapter 22).

However, there are also other arguments for monopolies not necessarily being against the consumer's best interests. When Sky TV was forced to share its Premier League screening rights with Setanta, many viewers were faced either with paying for two subscriptions or losing the viewing rights to some of the games. Suddenly it seemed better to have a sole, monopoly supplier than two companies competing with each other.

There is also the case of **natural monopoly**. Where providing a service requires the construction and maintenance of expensive infrastructure, one business is often better than two or more. Two businesses building train tracks from London to Birmingham would double the disruption and the construction and maintenance costs. Each business may get half the customers but this is unlikely to pay enough to cover the companies' costs unless prices are higher than if there had been just one railway company.

Additionally, it is often better to have one company when public safety is important. For example, two companies trying to get the business of processing used nuclear material might be tempted to cut costs to get a competitive

The Science Bit

Monopolies can also occur when there are several companies in the market. In this case the companies work together and basically act as one larger company with fixed prices or restricted supply to drive prices up. This is known as **collusion**. It is illegal, but year after year of successful prosecutions shows that it still happens quite regularly in Britain and elsewhere.

edge over their rival – and the results could be disastrous.

Conclusion

Monopolists have the power to influence the market in which they operate. They may offer poor quality at high prices and be lazy when it comes to innovating. However, remember that where large infrastructure is required, the economy may be better off with a monopoly provider.

Talking Point

Can market control be measured? What makes one company a monopolist and another not?

Revision Essentials

Collusion – where several firms act together to effectively become a monopoly.

Monopoly – where a single supplier dominates the sales in a market and therefore has a degree of control over it.

Natural monopoly – where market conditions mean that it is in everyone's best interest for a business to be in a monopoly position.

Exercises

(A and B: 15 marks; 30 minutes)

A1. State the meaning of the term 'monopoly'. (2)

2. Describe a market where you believe there is a company that has a monopoly. Give reasons why you believe the company is a monopoly. (3)

3. Explain a situation where a monopoly could be good for consumers. (4)

B In 2001, the telephone numbers 118 118, 118 500 and the other enquiry numbers did not exist in the UK. Instead, there was one provider called Directory Enquiries, which was dialed using 192, and which was run by British Telecom. At the time, the market was valued at over £250m.

Promotion for 118

1. Suggest three reasons why the Government decided to break up the monopoly that Directory Enquiries (192) enjoyed. Explain each reason. (6)

Classroom Activity

(Groups of 2–4; 30 minutes)

In many schools, a monopoly exists: the school canteen! In your groups discuss the following points:

● Is your school canteen a monopoly? Why/why not?
● Assuming a monopoly does exist, what are the benefits and costs of this to the students of the school?

Practice Questions

Guernsey is an island covering 30 square kilometres situated in the English Channel. 'Guernsey Post' is the only provider of postal services on the island. It is currently under threat from an investigation by the competition authorities. The business argues that it wants to increase its charges but this has been met with resistance and the claim that it is time to shake up the postal market on the island.

Questions

(15 marks; 25 minutes)

1 Which one of the following is a benefit of monopoly? (2)

  a) There is more choice of products and services.

  b) They can reduce costs by buying in bulk.

  c) Prices will be lower.

2 How might having more than one postal business improve the market for postal services in Guernsey? Explain at least two benefits. (4)

3 Guernsey Post claims that new competition would lead to an unequal level of service across the island, with new companies choosing the areas where the costs of delivery may be lower.

  Using your knowledge of costs and benefits of monopoly, consider the effects of allowing the postal monopoly to remain in Guernsey. (9)

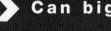

Chapter 22

Regulation

After the credit crunch led to falling demand in 2008, the media were quick to point the finger of blame at the Government. The creation of complicated financial systems that too few could understand had led to loans being made by banks that were in no position to carry on lending. Journalists claimed that the Government should have had **regulation** outlawing over-complicated investments. The banks, however, had always argued that regulation is time consuming and reduces innovation. Before the 'crunch', people had accepted the idea that the banks knew best, so regulation was unnecessary. The crunch revealed the hollowness of the bankers' claims.

What can regulation do?

Regulation exists to prevent businesses from exploiting their control of a market. It may take the form of:

- price controls, so that businesses cannot impose unreasonable prices
- setting minimum quality standards, backed by ways to complain if customers are treated unfairly.
- preventing businesses acting in socially unacceptable ways. For example, preventing city-centre bars and nightclubs promoting binge-drinking by offering deals such as 'all you can drink for £10'
- ensuring businesses provide a service for needy customers such as those in remote areas, even though there isn't a great deal of profit from doing so.

Those who don't follow the rules could find themselves having to pay large fines or having their market-share restricted by being forced to sell part of their business.

What is the right amount of regulation?

No regulation?

A complete lack of regulation of businesses would leave consumers very vulnerable. Without regulation there would be no requirement for a business to offer a warranty on goods. In the long term, companies may build up a positive reputation but along the way dishonest businesses would 'rip off' customers and might endanger customer safety. Businesses in a monopoly would be able to do completely as they pleased.

Self-regulation?

A business (or a group of businesses) may agree to **self-regulation.** A code of conduct will be put together that businesses will agree to follow. Businesses prefer this as they can choose the regulation – and possibly the punishments themselves. However, because it is self-regulation, there is *no legal requirement* for them to do so. If one business chooses to ignore the rules, they can't be punished for doing so.

Government regulation?

The Government may create laws that force businesses to act in a certain way. Complying with such laws is compulsory so if the Government is effective this should guarantee that consumers are protected. However, businesses complain that the Government may not fully understand the market. They say that regulation is time consuming, expensive and often reduces their competitiveness. This creates negative effects on customers, such as unnecessarily high prices.

In the UK, competition laws are enforced by the **Competition Commission.** They are often asked to pass judgement on proposed takeovers and mergers where two businesses come together to form one larger one. By joining together, businesses can build up too much market control so the Competition Commission can prevent them from doing so.

The Science Bit

When regulation failed to prevent massive fraud by Enron in 2001, the US Government introduced the Sarbanes-Oxley Act, which forced large companies to report the tiniest of details about their financial activities. Companies reported that it was costing them $1.7m each year just to meet the requirements of the Act but it *has* reduced investors' uncertainty over fraud.

Conclusion

Consumers are vulnerable to businesses that have a degree of control over a market. Businesses prefer to regulate themselves but they are tempted to do as little as possible to keep customers happy. The Government can get involved but are criticised for slowing businesses down and costing them extra money, which can end up hurting customers. The best solution is ensuring there is proper competition in the market. Competitive businesses will always try to provide a better service for customers in order to survive and earn bigger profits.

Talking Point

Some businesses have been accused of deliberately breaking the law because the fines they incur in doing so are smaller than the extra profits they have gained. How should governments decide how large the fines should be?

Revision Essentials

Competition Commission – a UK and EU government organisation that prevents businesses taking advantage of their market position.

Government regulation – where the Government uses laws and punishments to influence how the businesses behave.

Self-regulation – where companies voluntarily agree to create and follow their own code of conduct.

Exercises

(A and B: 14 marks; 30 minutes)

A1. Explain the meaning of the term 'self-regulation'. (2)

2. Explain three reasons why a monopoly might need to be regulated. (6)

B In 2009 the European Commission charged a number of technology manufacturers with fixing the prices of LCD television screens. The group of companies was accused of acting together to keep prices high to increase profit.

Adapted from: *The Guardian*, 13 July 2009

1. Explain what is meant by 'price fixing'. (2)

2. Explain how the intervention of the European Commission attempted to ensure a better deal for customers. (4)

Classroom Activity

(Groups of 3–4; 40 minutes)

Use the internet to research one of the following:

- the European Commission investigation into elevator manufacturers
- the Office of Fair Trading investigation into Tesco and Morrisons
- the Competition Commission's investigation into the Holland and Barrett/Julian Graves merger.

Produce a three-minute presentation that summarises why these business were being investigated. Discuss the impact on consumers and the businesses concerned.

Practice Questions

In 2004 a government report set out ways to tackle child obesity. It included a review of the advertising, sponsorship and promotion of food and drink to consumers. The report stated that advertisers needed to be more responsible (in terms of communication with children) or face regulation. In response, Coca-Cola continued a strong process of self-regulation. They do not advertise to under-12s. This includes ensuring broadcast times are appropriate and that they do not advertise on channels aimed at children and do not use celebrities who are well known to children.

In addition, Coca-Cola has continued to develop more health-orientated products such as juices and low- or no-calorie drinks. They have improved labelling on packaging and are encouraging teenagers to get active through sports programmes.

Questions

(10 marks; 25 minutes)

1 Explain why Coca-Cola would prefer the route of self-regulation. (4)

2 To what extent do you think self-regulation by companies such as Coca-Cola will succeed in reducing businesses exploiting their market power? (6)

Chapter 23

Pressure groups

In 1990 Chris Hines set up a group called Surfers Against Sewage (SAS). His aim was to put pressure on the businesses responsible for polluting coastal waters so that they would clean up their act. In just seven months SAS had 2,000 members and Chris enjoyed extensive media coverage. SAS persuaded Brighton council to prevent South West Water only building a basic sewage treatment works. By 2006 SAS had played a key role in the EU agreeing to create regulation protecting bathing water.

Chris Hines would never have managed to force businesses to change their ways on his own. By forming a **pressure group** he was able to make the businesses take notice of his complaints and protect the interests of those who use the coastal waters. Being part of a larger group means you are more likely to change the behaviour of a business.

What can pressure groups do?

Pressure groups try to promote their cause in a number of ways:

- publicising any wrongdoing by businesses in an effort to damage their reputation and threaten their profit

- writing to members of parliament or the council asking them to take action

- organising protests, demonstrations and petitions

- persuading people not to use the business in the future. This is known as a 'boycott'

- direct action to disrupt the activities of the business. This may include illegal activities such as blocking gates or trespassing.

The internet has made it much easier for pressure groups to organise themselves and get their message heard. Greenpeace, for example, has its own channel on YouTube. Facebook groups and Tweets can also create an upsurge of pressure upon a business or on government.

Do businesses respond to pressure groups?

The answer depends on a few factors. These are:

- *The credibility of the pressure group*. Where pressure groups lack statistics or facts to back up their argument, businesses can legitimately ignore them. Also, pressure groups that regularly break the law in direct action can be overlooked as a result of their poor behaviour.

- *Where the customers are located*. If a local pressure group in Ghana complains that a factory is damaging the local environment, will British customers find out? Will they even care?

- *The number of rival businesses*. A business with market control may care very little if a pressure group damages its reputation because customers have no alternatives.

- **The type of business**. A big brand will be damaged by negative publicity but a small manufacturing firm is less likely to be affected.

The Science Bit

Businesses are keen to portray a positive image to avoid the attention of pressure groups. Many do this by creating a **Corporate Social Responsibility** (CSR) policy that is a commitment to exceed the basic legal requirement to their stakeholders. It may be, though, that the focus of the CSR policy is really on publicity (public relations) rather than on any major changes in how the company carries out its activities.

Conclusion

Well-organised pressure groups can be a serious force against businesses who neglect their stakeholders. Businesses with a hard-earned reputation have a lot to lose against pressure groups that are angry about the damage a business is doing. However, the ability of pressure groups to succeed is limited by consumers' interest in the story. Often, 'out of sight is out of mind'.

Talking Point

Consider 'The Science Bit.' Do you think oil companies that create CSR policies genuinely care about their stakeholders or do they create these just to avoid the disruption caused by pressure groups?

Revision Essentials

Corporate Social Responsibility – a policy to convince the stakeholders in a business that its actions are in the best interests of society, not just those of its shareholders.

Pressure group – an organisation set up to influence businesses and government to protect stakeholders.

Exercises

(A and B: 17 marks; 35 minutes)

A1. Explain what is meant by the term 'pressure group'. (3)

2. State four examples of pressure groups that you are familiar with and describe their cause. (4)

B   www.tescopoly.org is a website coordinated by organisations concerned about the power of Tesco. They believe that the continued growth of Tesco is having negative consequences on a number of stakeholders.

1. a) State two stakeholders you believe the website would represent.

    b) Explain why they are stakeholders in the growth of Tesco. (4)

    A recent Tesco advert promotes an offer for children's school clothing, where parents can purchase a coat, shoes, two shirts, and two skirts or trousers for £15.

2. Explain why Tesco's customers' views might not be the same as those of Tescopoly. (6)

Classroom Activity

(Groups of 3–4, 30 minutes)

Greenpeace protest against the expansion of Heathrow

Greenpeace is one of the major pressure groups fighting the expansion of airports, particularly Heathrow. Working in groups, consider if pressure groups can be effective in making businesses consider their stakeholders more thoughtfully.

Practice Questions

Pressure groups have taken an interest in Nestlé since the 1980s. They believed that the food giant had been marketing baby milk unethically. They argue that in many developing countries mothers do not have a consistent supply of clean water and electricity to mix and heat the powder with, which places babies in danger.

Nestlé's website clearly outlines their support of breast-feeding, but also outlines the argument that when mothers choose not to breastfeed their baby milk is the only one recognised by the World Health Organisation. They also have a code of conduct for their work in developing countries.

Questions

(12 marks; 35 minutes)

1 Explain how pressure groups are stakeholders. (4)

2 To what extent do you believe that pressure groups prevent the exploitation of stakeholders. Use examples to illustrate your answer. (8)

IS GROWTH GOOD?

Chapter 24

Gross domestic product

In 2008 the United States of America had the largest economy in the world according to the World Bank. In fact, the US economy was nearly three times as big as that of Japan (which was listed in second place). The US economy was over five times bigger than the UK's.

Economists measure the size of economies by calculating the value of all the products and services produced in the economy over a period of time. The value of this is known as **gross domestic product (GDP).** So America's GDP is over five times the size of the UK's.

Economic growth

An increase in GDP over time means that the economy is producing more than it used to. When this is the case, economists say there is **economic growth.** Economists usually measure this every quarter (three months) of a year.

Table 1: Example of GDP over time

Time period	Gross domestic product (billion sovereigns)	Economic growth from last quarter (%)	Economic growth from last year (%)
Jan–Mar 2009	100		
Apr–Jun 2009	102.1	+2.1%	
July–Sep 2009	104.5	+2.4%	
Oct –Dec 2009	105.8	+1.2%	
Jan–Mar 2010	105.4	–0.4%	+5.4%
Apr–Jun 2010	104.1	–1.2%	+2.0%

Table 1 shows the GDP of an economy. The last column shows how much GDP has increased compared with the same period the year before. The increase in GDP from 100 to 105.4 billion sovereigns is economic growth of 5.4 per cent.

Small percentages of economic growth are worth billions of dollars (or pounds or euros) of extra production so should not be overlooked. In fact, economic growth above 3 per cent is spectacular for most economies because they don't have the capacity to grow that fast. Normally, only countries with huge unfulfilled potential can grow above 3 per cent a year.

Negative economic growth is quite rare. No more than 5 of the last 50 years have had negative growth. When there is less produced this quarter compared with the last one, the economy is shrinking and there is negative economic growth.

Why does economic growth happen?

Economic growth can occur for three reasons:

- **Investment in new factories and machinery.** Up-to-date facilities mean more can be produced in a given time.
- **Education.** A well-educated and well-trained workforce will produce more valuable products, faster than before.
- **Investment in infrastructure such as roads and communication.** If the Government provides faster trains or faster broadband speeds, businesses can be more efficient and produce more.

These factors will all increase the amount the economy *can* produce. Remember that businesses will only produce more if people *want more*. But as explained in Chapter 1, people seem to have limitless wants! So, as long as the economy is capable of producing more, there will probably be a market for that extra production.

The Science Bit

Economic growth data shown on a graph can often catch students out.

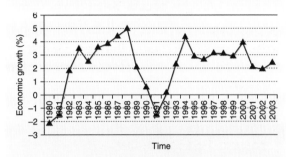

Changes in demand over time
Source: Figures from www.measuringworth. org/

When the line is moving downward (e.g. between 2000 and 2001) it doesn't mean that the economy is shrinking. Instead, it means that the economy is growing but at a slower rate than previously. Only when economic growth is less than zero (e.g. between 1980 and 1981 and in 1991) is the economy shrinking.

Conclusion

The gross domestic product shows the value of the products and services produced in the economy. Economic growth shows the percentage increase in GDP over a period (normally a quarter of one year). Small percentages of economic growth each quarter quickly add up to large increases in the amount produced in an economy over a period of time.

Talking Point

Why do you think it is easier for a developing country to achieve higher percentages of economic growth?

Revision Essentials

Economic growth – occurs when gross domestic product increases from one period of time to another. It is shown as a percentage.

Gross Domestic Product – the measure of the value of goods and services produced in an economy over a period of time.

Exercises

(A and B: 23 marks; 40 minutes)

A1. State what GDP stands for and what it measures. (2)

2. What advantages are there from comparing countries using GDP per capita, rather than simply GDP? (3)

3. Examine whether a country with a high GDP must always have a high standard of living. (6)

B1. The table shows the amount of GDP in the UK over time. Use this information to answer the following questions:

Year; Quarter 1	£m
2000	274,170
2001	282,599
2002	287,685
2003	294,236
2004	304,784
2005	310,313
2006	320,125
2007	327,872
2008	336,042
2009	319,512

a) Calculate the percentage change in GDP from 2007–08. (2)

b) What does this tell you about the UK economy? (3)

c) Calculate the percentage change in GDP from 2008–09. (2)

d) What does this tell you about the UK economy? (3)

2. What would you expect to happen to GDP when there is reduced demand? (2)

Classroom Activity

(Groups of 3–4; 40 minutes)

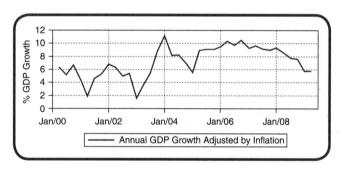

India GDP growth rate
Source: India Central Statistical Organization

The chart shows annual GDP growth for India. In groups of three, discuss the following points and prepare a presentation for the rest of the class, showcasing your views.

● The reasons for the rapid rise in growth between 2003 and 2004.

● The reasons for the fall in growth from 2007 to 2008.

● Which reasons you feel are the most significant in explaining these changes.

You might find the following websites helpful in your investigation:

www.bbc.co.uk/news

www.guardian.co.uk

www.cia.gov

Practice Questions

Questions

(13 marks; 30 minutes)

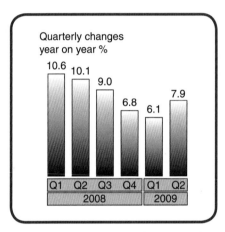

Quarterly changes
year on year %

China GDP. Source: China NBS

1 Which one of the following statements is correct, relating to the graph showing China's
   GDP? (1)

   a) China's GDP fell between Q1 in 2008 and Q1 2009.
   b) China's GDP has fallen at a consistent rate during 2008.
   c) China's GDP continued to rise during 2008 but at a falling rate.

2 Suggest and explain two reasons for the high levels of economic growth in China. (6)

3 Analyse the impact that falling economic growth would have on the Chinese economy.
   (6)

Chapter 25

Standard of living

In 2006 Iceland was considered the 'best' place to live in the world by the **Human Development Index (HDI).** The United Nations (UN) publishes the HDI league table every year. Those living in countries at the top are considered to have the best overall **standard of living.** Those at the bottom are considered to have the worst. If Iceland is the best place to live, the central African countries of Burkina Faso and Sierra Leone are apparently the worst.

What is standard of living?

In Chapter 24 we saw that the United States of America has the biggest economy in terms of value of items (or income) produced. If it has the most income surely it is the 'best' place to live? Not necessarily as table 1 shows.

Table 1 Measures of standards of living

	GDP (nominal US $) 2008		GDP per capita (PPP) 2008		HDI Index (2006)	
1	United States	14,204,322	Luxembourg	78,559	Iceland	0.968
2	Japan	4,909,272	Norway	58,141	Norway	0.968
3	People's Republic	3,860,039	Singapore	49,288	Canada	0.967
4	Germany	3,652,824	United States	46,716	Australia	0.965
5	France	2,853,062b	Ireland	44,195	Ireland	0.96
6	United Kingdom	2,645,593	Switzerland	42,534	Netherlands	0.958
7	Italy	2,293,008	Netherlands	40,850	Sweden	0.958
8	Brazil	1,612,539	Austria	38,153	Japan	0.956
9	Russia	1,607,816	Sweden	37,383	Luxembourg	0.956
10	Spain	1,604,174	Iceland	36,770	Switzerland	0.955
11	Canada	1,400,091	Denmark	36,604	France	0.955
12	India	1,217,490	Canada	36,444	Finland	0.954
13	Mexico	1,085,951	Australia	35,677	Denmark	0.952
14	Australia	1,015,217	Germany	35,613	Austria	0.951
15	South Korea	929,121	United Kingdom	35,445	United States	0.95

	GDP (nominal US $) 2008		GDP per capita (PPP) 2008		HDI Index (2006)	
16	Netherlands	860,336	Finland	35,426	Spain	0.949
17	Turkey	794,228	Belgium	34,493	Belgium	0.948
18	Poland	526,966	Japan	34,099	Greece	0.947
19	Indonesia	514,389	France	34,045	Italy	0.945
20	Belgium	497,586	Equatorial Guinea	33,883	New Zealand	0.944

Source: World Bank/UN Human Development Report Programme (Statistical Update)

You have to remember that although the USA has the highest total income (Gross Domestic Product or GDP) in the world, it also has the world's third largest population to share that income among. To take this into account economists divide the income of a country by its population to give **GDP per capita** (per person). This sees the US drop to 4th, while the UK drops from 6th to 15th.

Even GDP per capita isn't a foolproof method of measuring everyone's standard of living. While it does divide up incomes, it doesn't mean that everyone gets an equal share.

Economists strive to see how fairly the income of an economy is distributed around the population.

This is known as **distribution of income.** As you can see from the red and pink areas in the map below, in South American countries as well as parts of Africa the income is very unfairly distributed. There may be high GDP per capita on average but it isn't equally shared around; few are enjoying most of the economy's income leaving the others with a very poor standard of living.

The UN tries to look at other factors that affect standard of living when creating the HDI. It looks at GDP and population as well as three other factors:

- *life expectancy* (the average number of years an individual is expected to live at birth).

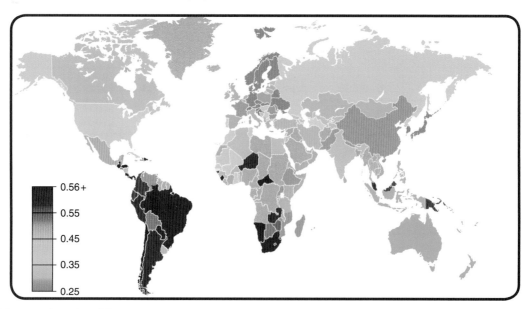

0.56+
0.55
0.45
0.35
0.25

World map showing GDP per capita
Source: UN Human Development Report Programme (Statistical Update)

This is a good estimate of the health care the population will receive

- *literacy rates* (the number of people who can read and write)
- *the number of years of education* that an individual receives.

The UN believes that life expectancy and literacy are good measures of the general quality of life the average person will receive. A high score in the HDI is supposed to represent a high standard of living for the average person.

Others believe that the HDI doesn't go far enough, because it doesn't include factors such as crime, environmental damage, religious freedom and freedom of speech. However, including so many variables would be very difficult.

The Science Bit

The Economist newspaper publishes a 'Quality of Life' Index, which is put together by its intelligence unit. It tries to include more variables than the HDI such as: family life, community values, climate, political stability, job security and gender equality. Ireland came top in a recent report.

Conclusion

Standard of living can be measured in several ways. If a country has a higher income (GDP) than another one you can argue that its standard of living should be higher as there are more products and services to enjoy. However, you also have to consider how many people are in the economy (GDP per capita) and how the products and services are distributed among the population (income distribution). However, even these methods don't take factors such as life expectancy and education into account. To do this, economists use the Human Development Index.

Talking Point

Using the information in this chapter, think about which country you would prefer to live in.

Revision Essentials

Standard of living – how economists look at an individual's share of the national income.

GDP per capita – the amount of income the country has overall, divided by its population to give the income per person.

Human Development Index – the United Nations' measure of standard of living. It includes GDP per capita as well as education and health care.

Distribution of income – how the national income is shared among the population. It can reveal if very few take the majority of the income or if it is shared equally.

Exercises

(A and B: 17 Marks; 35 minutes)

A1. In your own words describe what is meant by GDP. (2)

2. Other than GDP, state three other ways to measure a country's standard of living. (3)

3. Of the four measures you have considered (including GDP), evaluate their effectiveness in providing an accurate way of comparing standards of living in different countries. (6)

B A recent article in *The Guardian* highlights that in 2009 the number of jobs lost is more than in any other year since the Second World War. Some measures show that Detroit's unemployment levels have reached 45 per cent.

Source: *The Guardian*, 20 December 2009

1. Describe two consequences of the high unemployment levels in Detroit. (2)

2. Explain how high unemployment can affect standard of living. (4)

Classroom Activity

(Groups of 2; 40 minutes)

Go to www.worldmapper.org and look at the different map categories. Consider how the world map looks different when different measures are selected. For example, try looking at the map for income and compare it to the one at the weblink below for infant mortality.

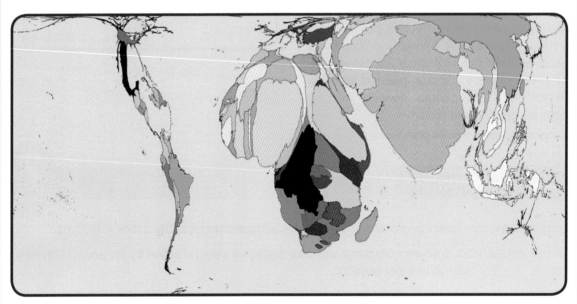

Map showing global infant mortality
Source: http://www.worldmapper.org/display.php?selected=261

Choose four different measures that you feel give an idea about the standard of living in that country. Using the maps to help you, report back to the class on which countries you think have the highest and lowest standards of living.

Do your classmates agree?

Practice Questions

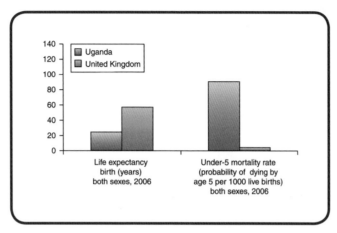

UK and Uganda; a comparison of the chances
of survival from birth in 2006
Source: World Health Organisation

Questions

(16 marks; 30 minutes)

1 What is the under-5 years mortality rate in the UK and Uganda in 2006? Use your own words to describe this statistic. (3)

2 Suggest two reasons why the mortality rate is higher in Uganda than in the UK. (2)

3 In 2006 the GDP per capita for these two countries were as follows:

UK	$38,849.97
Uganda	$312.04

Explain what these figures show. (3)

4 Calculate the GDP per capita of Uganda as a percentage of that of the UK. (2)

5 Suggest and explain two ways in which GDP per capita in Uganda could be increased. (6)

Chapter 26

The benefits and drawbacks of growth

In October 2009 NASA published the photograph below.

The grey haze isn't cloud: it's air pollution trapped under warmer air. China's rapid economic growth has had several benefits but has also brought costs such as environmental damage. China's case isn't a one-off; every economy must try and balance the benefits and drawbacks of economic growth.

Benefits of economic growth

Economic growth creates extra income for an economy. Even if this isn't shared equally among the population it has benefited at least one person. As long as that one person's extra income hasn't harmed anyone else, the whole economy is a little better off.

Over a period of years, though, economic growth can bring a society from poverty to comfort. In 1979, China was a country in which famine was a real possibility if the rice harvest failed. Thirty years later the Chinese Government was worrying about traffic jams and obesity, not starvation.

There are also other benefits of economic growth. A wealthier economy is more able to invest in essentials such as roads and hospitals (infrastructure). This investment may:

- limit the damage caused by further economic growth, e.g. investing in recycling schemes
- provide the economy with the ability to trade with other countries
- give an economy the strength to overcome difficult events such as a natural disaster.

Drawbacks of economic growth

Economic growth puts pressure on the resources in an economy. Economic growth requires more resources (particularly energy) to be used to produce the extra goods and services required. Non-renewable resources such as copper and oil will run out faster. As they become scarcer, their price will skyrocket – causing more uncertainty and damage to the economy.

Table 1 Depletion of non-renewable resources

Longevity of resources at current consumption levels
Aluminium: 131 years
Coal: 150 years
Copper: 31 years
Gold: 17 years
Iron: 79 years
Natural gas: 64 years
Petroleum: 42 years
Silver: 13 years
Tin: 17 years

Source: *Science et Vie,* June 2008

The desire to produce more and more also puts a strain on the environment. Along with the depletion of non-renewable resources (see Table 1) there is also the pollution associated with power stations, factories and transport. Busier towns also suffer from congestion, while farmers may become tempted to use dangerous pesticides to get more intensive crops.

There can also be a social cost of economic growth. In order to support continued growth in China, the Government has built the Three Gorges Hydroelectric Dam across the Yangtze River. This has flooded archaeological and cultural sites and the homes of 1.24 million people. Homelessness as a result of a government project is an extreme cost of economic growth; however, there is also research linking growth with 'deterioration in the quality of our lives'.

Is it worth it?

Increased economic growth today will be enjoyed by the current population and create a wealthier platform for future generations. However, rapid growth today could also mean that future generations are left without important resources or a fragile and damaged environment. Is it right for us to enjoy the planet at the expense of future generations?

The Science Bit

It is very difficult to forecast the damage that today's actions will have on future generations. We know there is plenty of oil available underground, but at the moment a lot of it is too expensive to extract. If a technology is developed to extract it cheaply there will be enough for several more years than is currently predicted. However, with these uncertainties we can't calculate the cost of today's economic growth on future generations.

Conclusion

Economic growth increases income and opportunities for future development, which is ultimately a good thing. However, if growth causes long-term damage to the environment, society must decide whether to stop pursuing growth at the expense of future generations.

Talking Point

According to predictions, China will overtake the US as the world's largest economy in 2035. What will be the main problems that China faces in the future?

Revision Essentials

Benefits of economic growth	Drawbacks of economic growth
• Increased income • Potentially more international trade • Allows development of new technology (for further growth without environmental damage?)	• Income may not be fairly distributed • Resource depletion • Pollution • Congestion • Social costs • Unfair on future generations?

Exercises

(A and B: 22 marks; 40 minutes)

A1. Copy and complete the following table. Try to think of as many different factors as possible. (6)

Positive effects of growth	Negative effects of growth

2. Select two of the negative effects of economic growth. Describe how these effects might continue to have negative impacts on society in the future. (6)

B   In 2008 Britain's economy reduced in size by 5.6 per cent, the steepest decrease since the 1930s. Source: *The Guardian*, 24 July 2009.

1. Explain the meaning of 'contraction in growth'. (4)

2. Describe how negative growth might impact on households in the UK. (6)

Classroom Activity

(Groups of 3–4; 35 minutes)

Wangari Maathai is the founder of the Green Belt movement and in 2004 she was awarded the 2004 Nobel Peace prize. When questioned about the impact of growth in Africa, she stated: 'We have limited resources, development must create a happy comfortable environment that gives us a good quality of life.'

In 2008, three African countries featured in *The Economist*'s list of fastest growing economies. Angola was first with 21.1 per cent economic growth.

You are going to take part in a class discussion. Teams must prepare arguments for and against the belief that growth in Africa is a good thing.

Practice Questions

During the G8 meeting that took place in late 2009, industrial countries agreed that by 2050 they would cut their carbon emissions by 80 per cent, with the aim of reducing global warming.

Other countries did not welcome the decision. Brazil cuts down trees in the Amazon, which would absorb 700m tonnes of carbon dioxide from the air every year. Brazil wants to reduce deforestation but like other countries they are not happy that other countries are telling them what to do.

Shyam Saran, who is the head of India's international negotiating team on climate change, explained that India will only accept a limit on their greenhouse gas emissions that is the same as that given to developed countries (on a per head basis).

Many believe that if developing countries do nothing then the efforts of the developed world will be wasted.

Questions

(14 marks; 30 minutes)

1 Describe two key benefits of economic growth to developing countries such as India and Brazil (4)

2 Explain how economic growth today could bring further benefits in the future. (6)

3 Apart from climate change what other problems might result from high levels of economic growth? (4)

Chapter 27

Renewable resources

In 2006 the World Wildlife Fund (WWF) published the *Living Planet Report*. It predicted that if the worldwide economy grows at the forecasted rate there will be 'total resource depletion and ecosystem collapse before 2050'. The WWF hopes that its report will make individuals, businesses and governments think more carefully and try to achieve **sustainable growth.**

What is sustainable growth?

An economy that is growing sustainably is one that is meeting the needs of current generations while preserving the environment so that future generations can meet their needs. The WWF believes current economic growth is causing so much pollution and environmental damage that future generations may struggle to achieve a good standard of living. This means it is unsustainable. Several other organisations also believe that climate change is an example of unsustainable growth. Our use of resources today will damage the environment for future generations.

Economists know that economic growth requires extra resources. Some resources such as iron ore are essential but non-renewable (they cannot be replaced). When they are getting used up, what is left will become increasingly scarce and eventually run out. The opportunity cost of using the last few tonnes of the materials to make steel will be huge if there are no alternatives. Should the last few pieces of steel go to building extra housing or new

hospitals? And when it's finally gone, how will we build anything without it?

Renewable resources would, in theory, solve this problem. Renewable resources are recreated by the environment at least as fast as we can use them. Replanting one tree for every tree cut down would result in a renewable supply of paper and timber. Renewable energy from wind turbines, solar power, hydroelectric dams and biomass could replace oil, gas and coal, meaning that the economy should always have a supply of energy.

Are renewable resources the answer?

Renewable resources certainly allow for growth that is *more* sustainable. If resources do not run out and are easily replaced, the economy can use them today without reducing their availability in the future.

However, renewable resources do not automatically mean that economic growth is totally sustainable. There are four reasons for this:

● *Huge investment*. The technology required to harvest renewable resources is often very expensive. Toyota Prius hybrid cars are more expensive than standard cars and are often criticised because the production of the batteries used to store electrical charge requires lots of energy and specialist resources.

- *Not all resources are renewable*. Precious materials such as gold and diamonds contribute to standards of living and cannot be replaced by new alternatives. Building materials like stone and steel are also non-renewable.
- *Increasing populations*. More demand for resources for an increased population may mean that although some resources are renewable they aren't replaced fast enough, particularly as more land is taken up for housing.
- *Environmental damage*. Producing renewable resources may, in itself, have harmful effects on the environment. For example, in Brazil farmers have planted so much of the same crop in an attempt to produce biofuel that they have damaged the ecosystem around them.

The Science Bit

Sustainable growth can be achieved through better use of non-renewable resources. Car manufacturers are now able to get cars to travel the same distance using less fuel than ever before. Fewer non-renewable resources are wasted, meaning that they will be less scarce in the future. It also gives scientists longer to come up with renewable alternatives.

Conclusion

The sustainability of economic growth is a hot topic. Renewable resources have a major role to play as they can be used without there being less for future generations. However, they do not solve all the problems of economic growth and must be used alongside other measures to make economic growth sustainable.

Talking Point

What role can recycling play in sustainable growth?

Revision Essentials

Renewable resources – resources that are recreated by the environment at least as fast as they are consumed.

Sustainable growth – a level of economic growth that meets the needs of current generations while preserving the environment so future generations can meet their needs.

Exercises

(A and B: 22 marks, 40 minutes)

A1. Explain the term 'sustainable growth'. (2)

2. List three resources that are non-renewable. (3)

3. List three resources that are renewable. (3)

B The UK Government is planning to install 10,000 new wind turbines by 2020. One of the proposed sites is a wind farm in Shetland. The scheme is set to cost £800m and, if approved, would generate 20 per cent of Scotland's domestic electricity. However, the scheme faces a petition signed by 21,000 residents and opposition from the Royal Society for the Protection of Birds and numerous heritage organisations. They claim the farm will ruin the landscape, damage breeding sites for rare birds and that installing the turbines could release significant carbon dioxide from the peat bogs below.

Adapted from: *The Guardian*, 28 July 2009

1. Produce a mind-map highlighting the benefits and drawbacks of building the wind farm in Scotland. (6)

2. Analyse two benefits and two drawbacks of using renewable resources. (8)

Classroom Activity

(Groups of 3 or 4; 40 minutes)

Shenzhen is in China, near the border with Hong Kong. It was originally a small fishing town. The area was declared a special economic zone in 1980 and by 2006 it had an economic growth rate of 31.2 per cent, according to Chinese economic data. Despite its high growth a report in the *New York Times* described Shenzhen as a model for a 'warning of the limitations of a growth-above-all approach'.

Quotation from *New York Times*, 19 December 2006

In your teams conduct some research about Shenzhen and build up a picture of the impact of high growth.

Practice Questions

Roland Berger, a firm of consultants, estimates that global spending on environmental technology is €1 trillion ($1.3 trillion) a year, and is set to grow.

A report in *The Economist* highlights that public investment in green technology brings costs as well as benefits. Taxpayers, for example, will ultimately have to pay for government spending in the form of higher taxes. Often too, spending on renewable electricity tends to raise the price of power, because wind and solar power plants cost more to build and run than coal-fired ones.

A study by Adam Rose and Dan Wei of Pennsylvania State University highlighted that increasing investment in renewable resources could impact on employment in coal mining, with 1.2m people put out of work. Gabriel Calzada Álvarez, a professor at King Juan Carlos University in Madrid, found that investment in renewable resources in Spain had led to 50,200 new jobs. Yet if the investment money had been given to private businesses, over double the number of jobs could have been created.

Adapted from: *The Economist,* 2 April 2009

Questions

(14 marks; 30 minutes)

1 Explain three reasons why governments are keen to invest in green technology. (6)

2 Apart from job losses in 'non-green' industries, analyse how investment in green technology may have negative effects. (8)

Chapter 28

Responsible businesses

Marks and Spencer launched their 'Plan A' in 2007. The retail giant set out a 100-point 'eco' plan that pledged to combat climate change, reduce waste, safeguard natural resources, trade ethically and build a healthier nation. Marks and Spencer have called it 'Plan A' "... because there is no plan 'B'". This is to suggest that the company believes that unless we act to protect the environment today there won't be another chance tomorrow.

Marks and Spencer's 'Plan A'

What responsibilities do businesses have?

Basic legal responsibilities

The **basic responsibilities** a business has to its stakeholders are laid out in laws created by the Government. For example, businesses must pay a minimum wage to its employees and dispose of waste according to rules and procedures. Not fulfilling these legal responsibilities means businesses would be punished with fines or even closure.

However, these laws are often basic requirements. Businesses can choose to go further than the basic requirement and make further contributions to society and the environment.

Social, environmental and ethical responsibilities

Some businesses see themselves as part of the local and global community, not just operating within it. This means that they feel a responsibility to act with the community in mind. Other firms see a commercial advantage in sounding 'green', especially those whose target market is environmentally conscious. But whether the motive is commercial or moral, the actions taken may be quite similar.

Businesses might choose to hold open days so the community can see the work they are doing.

Technology firms may offer free computer training to adults, or businesses with large meeting rooms may let them to community groups for free.

> As of 2009, accountancy firms KPMG and Deloitte allow every one of its staff at least one day per year to take part in charitable work. Tesco annually promotes and organises the 'Race for Life' to raise money for Cancer Research. Aston Villa Football Club gave up the opportunity for millions of pounds when it gave away its shirt sponsorship to the Acorns charity.

Businesses may get involved in more sophisticated recycling or energy saving than the law requires. They may also commit to being carbon neutral, which means for every tonne of greenhouse gas a business produces it will invest in projects that reduce greenhouse gases by a tonne.

Corporate Social Responsibility

Many businesses create plans that outline how they plan to exceed their minimum responsibilities to their stakeholders. Business leaders call these Corporate Social Responsibility (CSR) plans (as mentioned earlier in Chapter 23).

Any business that exceeds its basic requirements is better than one that does the bare minimum (or less). However, CSR is often criticised by pressure groups as just a device to make a business appear more attractive to its customers. They wonder if businesses genuinely care about the environment, communities and charities they engage with. Or, are they simply trying to gain a better image and a competitive edge over rivals?

In many companies, CSR is run within the Public Relations department; this gives a clear idea that it is about 'ticking boxes' with the public, rather than changing the way the business thinks and

acts. Environmental activists refer to 'greenwash', i.e. companies that whitewash their reputation by sprinkling some environmental imagery over their operations.

The Science Bit

When deciding whether to invest in a new technology to reduce pollution or waste, a business will consider how long it will take to get the money back. Converting a fleet of 1,000 vans to biofuel may cost £10,000. However, if it saves £2,500 a year, the investment will have paid for itself in four years *and* will have benefited the environment.

Conclusion

The Government puts basic requirements in place to prevent businesses exploiting their stakeholders. Some businesses choose to take on additional responsibilities for the environment and the community. The case of Aston Villa (giving sellable shirt space to charity) shows that some businesses do care. Others, however, act in line with their own sense of self-interest. That is understandable, but critics point out that 'greenwash' can tar all firms with the same brush – making consumers sceptical of all environmental claims made by businesses.

Talking Point

Apart from comparing CSR spending to the business's profits, can you think of other ways of finding out whether businesses act responsibly because they want to or because they feel they have to?

Revision Essentials

Basic responsibilities – measures put in place by the Government to prevent businesses damaging the environment and exploiting stakeholders.

Corporate Social Responsibility – a policy of a business to exceed its basic legal requirement to its stakeholders.

Exercises

(A and B: 22 marks; 40 minutes)

A1. Describe two ways in which a business could behave in a socially responsible way. (4)

2. Describe two ways in which a business could behave in a socially irresponsible way. (4)

3. Explain how different stakeholders may have different views about a company investing in social or environmental policies. (6)

B   In recent years Coca-Cola has often been the subject of criticism for its part in global water shortages. In 2007 they decided to work with the World Wildlife Fund to support water conservation. While the company still finds itself under the spotlight, this partnership has gone some way to restoring its image.

1. To what extent do you think Coca-Cola's motivation to form a partnership with the WWF was due to environmental concern? (8)

Classroom Activity

(Groups of 2; 60 minutes)

Several European businesses like Cadbury, Mars and Ikea claim to be investing in responsible activities such as using Fairtrade cocoa supplies and wood from responsibly managed forests.

With a partner, research two businesses and find out what they are doing to reduce their environmental impact or to improve their social impact. Produce a poster displaying your findings.

Practice Questions

Wolseley UK provides the widest range of construction products and materials in the UK. On a global scale they are the world's largest distributer of plumbing and heating products.

In 2002 Wolseley reviewed its social responsibility policies and conducted some market research. First, the company discovered that customers did not know much about sustainable building products and if they did, they did not know where to buy them.

Second, Wolseley found that the only businesses supplying sustainable building products were small, usually only operating within a tiny local area.

In 2008 the sustainable building centre was built in Leamington Spa, Warwickshire at a cost of £3.2m. The centre displayed the latest in building technology and provides information about 7,000 sustainable products that are available through Wolseley. Even before opening, over 100 visits to the centre had been scheduled and since opening in April 2008 there have been over 4,000 visitors.

Questions

(14 marks; 30 minutes)

1 Explain how Wolseley's sustainable building centre will encourage the use of more sustainable building products. (6)

2 To what extent was the policy to build the sustainable building centre a commitment to sustainable building? (8)

Chapter 29

Government intervention

In 1997 the UK Government encouraged the company LG to build a factory in Wales and create 6,000 jobs. The encouragement was financial, estimated to be worth £30,000 per job created. LG weren't the only lucky ones, with Siemens and Toshiba among several other businesses also rewarded for locating in Wales.

The growth of businesses and the economy brings benefits to some and costs to others. Large, successful businesses may locate in certain areas in order to get the most talented staff or benefit from transport links. This benefits one area (and pushes up wages of people who already have a job), but in other areas people may remain unemployed.

The Government has the responsibility to make sure that the benefits and costs are fair. When the Government gets involved in how the economy operates it is called **government intervention.** The Government gave incentives to businesses to locate in Wales in order to reduce unemployment so that the benefits of business and economic growth are shared fairly around the country.

The Government can intervene by:

- Taxing activities causing growth that benefits some at the expense of others. First, most governments place higher rates of income **tax** on those who earn the most in order to reduce the rates of tax placed on the less well-off. The

Government also taxes business profits and puts high taxes on activities that inflict costs on others, such as smoking or driving.
- Encouraging businesses to act in certain ways with financial incentives known as **subsidies.** For example, businesses may be given extra money for investing in green, eco-friendly technology or equipment.
- Creating rules (and laws) to ensure businesses act in ways that don't inflict costs on others as a result of their growth. Businesses that fail to comply with the **regulation** will face punishments such as fines or other restrictions.

The Science Bit

In 2005 the EU began a system of tradable permits for large businesses to produce greenhouse gases. If a large business wants to produce 'extra' greenhouse gases it must pay for a permit to do so. This means that the Government is taxing polluting behaviour in order to discourage it. Businesses that have invested in clean technologies (and so have spare permits) may sell their permits to 'dirty' businesses. So these 'clean' companies are, in effect, given a subsidy by the Government.

Conclusion

If left unchecked, individuals and businesses are often tempted to act selfishly and reap rewards for themselves at the expense of others. It is the Government's responsibility to make sure this doesn't happen and it can do so by using taxation, subsidies and legislation.

For more detail on government spending and taxation and regulation see Chapters 18 and 22.

Talking Point

Consider 'The Science Bit'. Is it right that businesses can buy their way out of damaging the environment? What are the alternatives?

Revision Essentials

Government intervention – when the Government uses taxation, subsidies or regulation to influence how businesses behave.

Regulation – when the Government uses laws and punishments to influence how businesses behave.

Subsidy – money provided by the Government as an incentive to individuals or businesses to act in a certain way.

Taxation – money raised by the Government by taking a slice of the income and spending of households and businesses.

Exercises

(A and B: 20 marks; 40 minutes)

A1. Match the term to the correct definition (3)

Term	Definition
Tax	An incentive paid by the Government to encourage businesses to produce more or in a certain way
Subsidy	Actions that control or restrict what a business can do. These may or may not be legally binding
Legislation	A charge placed on the consumption of a good or service

2. Describe a government subsidy you are familiar with. (2)

3. How might subsidies be more effective than taxes when encouraging businesses to act in an environmentally responsible way? (6)

B The Green Transport Plan, announced by the Government in 2005, meant that employers could loan money to employees to buy a bicycle. The idea was that employees use this bike for all or part of their commute to work. This would help to reduce the number of vehicles on the road and would therefore be more environmentally friendly. The loan was taken from company profits before they were taxed so there was a financial incentive for businesses to do this.

In 2004 the Environment Agency fined companies £2.3m for environmental offences, as well as prosecuting 20 individual company directors.

1. Explain how the bicycle scheme will benefit two stakeholders. (4)

2. To what extent will prosecuting individual company directors have a positive effect on business behavior? (5)

Classroom Activity

(Groups of 3–4; 40 minutes)

In 2007 Thames Water were fined £125,000 for one of Britain's worst pollution incidents. Industrial strength chlorine was released during a clean-up of a sewage plant. It took three days to clear two tonnes of dead fish from the river. Agencies criticised the size of the fine, which was equal to 0.1 per cent of Thames Water's annual revenue.

Adapted from; *The Guardian*, 27 January 2009

1. With your team use the internet to research fines that have been given to UK businesses for activities resulting in damage to the environment. Find out:

    a) how much the fine was

    b) what proportion the fine was of the company's annual revenue.

    Be ready to report back to the class.

Practice Questions

In 1997 John Prescott, the then Deputy Prime Minister declared: 'I will have failed if in five years' time there are not far fewer journeys by car.' Five years later, traffic had risen by 7 per cent.

The chart shows the increase of tax on unleaded petrol. Tax on fuel is politically unpopular; it is disliked by both businesses and individual consumers.

The amount of tax paid on petrol doesn't depend on income. This means a family with an income of £20,000 who drives 10,000 miles per year will find that a bigger proportion of its income goes on fuel than someone who drives the same miles but earns £100,000 per year. For this reason many people believe it is an unfair tax.

Despite these concerns, it is still important to make using cars less attractive because it will reduce congestion and have a real impact on the environment.

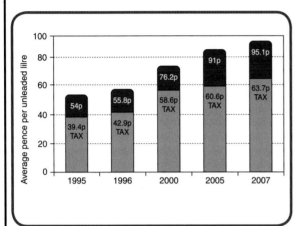

Cost of petrol per litre since 1995
Source: http://www.petrolprices.com

Questions

(15 marks; 30 minutes)

1 Which of the following is *not* a type of taxation imposed by the Government? (1)

   a) income tax

   b) student loan repayments

   c) VAT.

2 In 2007 what percentage of the price of fuel was tax? (2)

3 Analyse how increasing fuel tax in order to meet environmental targets will impact UK businesses. (6)

4 To what extent can governments protect the environment when their primary objective is to get re-elected? (6)

IS THE WORLD FAIR?

Absolute and relative poverty

In 2008 71 million American people did not have adequate health insurance. This means that if they became ill they would not be able to afford to pay for some or all of their treatment. Their medical care was funded by the Government and is very basic. Meanwhile the other 230 million American people would be treated to the highest standard of care available, courtesy of their private health insurance. So, were these 71 million people in poverty? Or just worse off than the 230 million others?

In many countries poverty means going hungry. In America or Britain that is rare, but in these countries many families are unable to find money for extras that they value highly. In America, that includes proper health care.

What does poverty mean?

- **Absolute poverty** is a situation where individuals do not have enough income to afford things required for an adequate standard of living, such as food, clothing and shelter. This means that their lives are constantly at risk.

- **Relative poverty** refers to a situation where individuals are not in absolute poverty. They are above the **poverty threshold** but cannot afford things considered 'normal' in their society. A person in the UK may be able to afford food and shelter but not have enough money for broadband internet or occasionally

going out. This means they may not be take a full part in society in the same way that others can. See Table 1 on the next page for further examples of these two types of poverty.

In every country in the world there is a degree of **inequality.** In other words some people are poorer than others. Therefore relative poverty exists everywhere. This becomes significant only if the degree of inequality is severe. When many people are struggling while others live a life of luxury, it is right to fear social problems. In countries where the latter is the situation, the rich often live in areas patrolled day and night by guards – perhaps armed ones.

Signs of poverty

The signs of poverty depend on whether or not the person is above or below the poverty line – see figure 1.

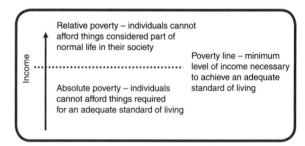

Figure 1 Above or below the poverty line?

Table 1 Signs of poverty

	Absolute	Relative
Food	Cannot afford to eat on a regular basis	Has to buy supermarket own-label food. Very rarely eats out
Shelter	Does not have a home capable of keeping out the wind and rain. No facilities for washing	Home is poorly decorated and chilly in winter but has basic washing facilities
Clothing	No access to basic clothing, particularly shoes	Has a selection of basic clothes and shoes but doesn't have 'nice' clothes for going out in
Health	Has no access to medicine, doctors and dentists	May have to wait to see a doctor or dentist
Social life	Spends all time trying to secure food and shelter	Has spare time to relax but cannot afford to buy cinema tickets, books, holidays, etc.
Communications	Has no access to TV, radio, internet or mobile phone	Has terrestrial TV but cannot afford Sky or Cable or a mobile phone or computer
Transport	Has no means to move between villages or towns	Can afford the bus but can't afford to run a car

Is there poverty in the UK?

Some people live in absolute poverty in the UK. There are homeless people in major towns and cities (particularly London). As a percentage of the whole population there are very few, but they must not be ignored given that they *are* living in absolute poverty.

There are many more people living in relative poverty in the UK, however. The children's charity Barnado's classes a child to be in relative poverty if they live in a household with less than 60 per cent of the average national household income. Using this measure they estimated that 3.9 million children (one in three) were living in relative poverty in 2009. Children living in relative poverty may have to wear shoes that they have grown out of, or have few toys or books to stimulate their minds.

Relative poverty among households isn't equally spread around the UK. In parts of London and Glasgow between 41 and 47 per cent of households are in relative poverty, while in other areas it is as low as 13 per cent.

The Science Bit

Economists try to consider the difference between income and wealth when investigating poverty. Around the UK there are lots of examples of retired people who live in large expensive houses, making them very wealthy but their retirement has meant that they now have very little income. So, although they live in a luxury house, in some ways they may be living in relative poverty because they can't afford to heat their home or go out with friends.

Conclusion

Millions of people around the world live in absolute poverty. Their access to basic things to survive is so limited that their lives are constantly endangered. In comparison, very few people in the UK live in absolute poverty. There is, however, inequality because there are people in the UK who cannot afford to live like the majority of society. These people are in relative poverty.

Talking Point

Why do you think there is regional variation in relative poverty in the UK?

Revision Essentials

Absolute poverty – where individuals cannot afford things required for an adequate standard of living.

Inequality – a word to describe the fact that there is relative poverty in a country or area.

Poverty threshold – the minimum level of income necessary to achieve an adequate standard of living.

Relative poverty – where individuals cannot afford things considered part of normal life in their society.

Exercises

(A and B: 16 marks, 20 minutes)

A1. In your own words, explain the meaning of the following terms:

a) Absolute poverty

b) Relative poverty. (4)

2. Do you believe there is absolute poverty in the UK? Explain your answer. (6)

B Look at the image and text below. Use the Revision Essentials to comment on the standard of living of this family. (6)

'By midday on Wednesday, Louise Spencer has £6.80 left in her purse to last until Monday, which works out at £1.36 a day to pay for anything she and her two small children might need. She is confident that she will make the money stretch. It's just a question of careful budgeting.

Providing a week's worth of meals for three people for £6.66 a head is easy once you work out how, she says. The gas and electricity payments for the week have already been made, so she knows the children will be warm. The only thing to fear is the unexpected – a broken pushchair, a request to buy her daughter's class photograph.

Louise, 24, doesn't smoke, drink or take drugs and she very rarely goes out with her friends. She spends pretty much all the money she gets in benefits on her children. She rejects the suggestion

that her family might be described as poor. "Oh no," she says firmly. "We get by."'

Source: 'A portrait of 21st-century poverty' by Amelia Gentleman, *The Guardian*, 18 March 2009

Classroom Activity

(Groups of 3-4; 45 minutes)

In your group find images of relative and absolute poverty. Create a poster that illustrates the differences between the two. You should use images from both developed and developing counties.

Practice Questions

The United Nations uses the Human Poverty Index to measure poverty. It takes into account non-financial elements of poverty such as life expectancy, adult literacy, water quality, and children who are underweight.

Highest and lowest Human Poverty Index scores

Rank	Territory	Value	Rank	Territory	Value
1	Burkina Faso	655	191	Japan	11.1
2	Niger	614	192	Spain	11.0
3	Mali	589	193	France	10.8
4	Ethiopia	555	194	Luxembourg	10.5

Rank	Territory	Value	Rank	Territory	Value
5	Zimbabwe	520	195	Germany	10.3
6	Zambia	504	196	Denmark	9.1
7	Mozambique	498	197	Finland	8.4
8	Chad	496	198	Netherlands	8.2
9	Mauritania	483	199	Norway	7.1
10	Guinea-Bissau	480	200	Sweden	6.5

Questions

(16 marks; 30 minutes)

1 Excluding the factors above, explain two other measures that you think could be used to determine whether there were high levels of poverty in a country. (4)

2 In the map on the left countries are shown by their geographical size (like normal maps). The map on the right shows countries in proportion of the number of people who live in an overcrowded household. The biggest country is the one with the most people living in an overcrowded house.

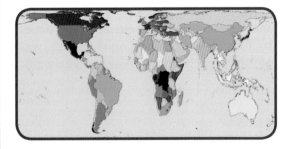

Countries by geographical size

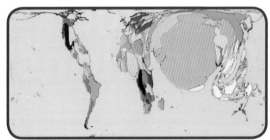

Countries in proportion of number of people living in an overcrowded household

Source: Worldmapper

a) Identify the two countries that have the highest numbers of people living in over-crowded conditions. (2)

b) In your opinion, would overcrowding lead to relative or absolute poverty? Explain your answer. (4)

3 The chart below shows the percentage of UK pensioners who live in poverty (defined as those who have less than 60 per cent of the average UK household income once they have paid for housing) according to their location.

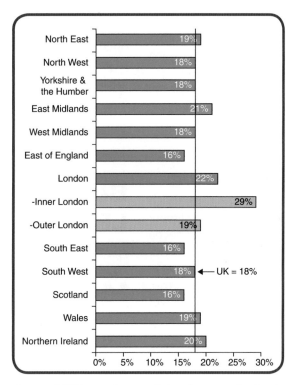

Percentage of UK pensioners living in poverty, by location

Source: House of Commons Library

a) How many areas of the country have more than the average number of pensioners living in poverty? (2)

b) Suggest two reasons why there might be higher levels of poverty among pensioners in this area. (4)

Chapter 31

International trade and LEDCs

The economies of different countries are blessed with different resources. The neighbouring countries of Ghana and Ivory Coast produce more cocoa than the rest of the world put together. Saudi Arabia supplies more oil than any other country, while Brazil produces twice as much sugar cane as the next biggest producer.

hy does trade happen?

Ghana and the Ivory Coast produce so much cocoa because they are good at it. Their climate is perfect for the growth of cocoa pods so cocoa grows much faster than anywhere else in the world. Also, their farmers have so much experience in producing cocoa that nobody else does it better. The same is true in Brazil, except their climate and knowledge favours sugar production.

We could produce both cocoa and sugar cane in the UK by building climate-controlled greenhouses and employing international specialists. But doing this would be more expensive than **importing** (buying) direct from Ghana and Brazil. Therefore this would be a waste of our resources. Instead, we put those resources into things we are good at: making processed foods such as biscuits and chocolate bars, or high-tech engineering such as Rolls-Royce aero-engines. Our expertise in manufacturing and engineering means we **export** (sell) it to other countries.

This is why **trade** happens. In exchange for cocoa and sugar cane, the UK can supply Ghana and Brazil with engineering products such as JCB excavators and diggers, which they are short of.

By trading the goods they're best at making, economies and people should benefit. They don't have to use extra resources producing something that another economy can do for less. Economists, therefore, like the idea of 'trade' because it should benefit everyone.

However, the impact of trade on some economies is less certain. Economies that are undeveloped and don't have the capacity or infrastructure to produce manufactured goods (and exist mainly on farming) are known as **Less Economically Developed Countries (LEDCs).** The effects of trade on LEDCs is not as clear as it is for more developed countries such as the UK.

Benefits of trade to LEDCs

LEDCs can in theory benefit from trade because:

- *it creates employment and increases skills.* Worldwide demand for products means that lots of people are required to meet the demand in the LECD. Through employment, workers develop their skills and enjoy their income
- *it encourages investment.* Satisfying the demands of other countries should generate extra profits for companies in the LEDCs. This extra profit allows businesses to invest in new technology and facilities.
- *it enables the country to access goods and technology they would otherwise not be able to.* Using the income generated from exporting their products, locals can import things from abroad.

Costs of trade to LEDCs

LEDCs can be damaged by trade because:

- *many less-developed countries export commodities such as copper or oil that are*

non-renewable. They may, therefore, be selling the country's prime assets. This is damaging if:

a) the commodities are sold too cheaply to foreign buyers who have a better understanding of their value, or

b) the commodities are sold, but the receipts end up in the Swiss bank accounts of corrupt leaders, instead of being used to build up the country's economy; some Western companies have been complicit in this type of theft.

- ***they can become dependent on one industry.*** Specialising in one item may be very rewarding if you are the world's leading economy at producing it. However, if the world decides it no longer wants it, or there is a problem producing it (such as a natural disaster) or another economy starts to produce it more cheaply, the economy will suffer much more than if it produced a variety of items.

The Science Bit

Fairtrade is an organisation that attempts to ensure that LEDCs only benefit from trade. The Fairtrade logo is a guarantee on a product that the local producers are paid no less than a fair minimum price for their supplies. In the UK, Cadbury has decided that all its Dairy Milk chocolate will come from Fairtrade suppliers (in Ghana).

Conclusion

In theory, trade should benefit everyone because it means goods would be produced in countries where they cost the least to make. Therefore everyone can enjoy them with the minimum of expense. In reality, this requires specialised production that may leave local people vulnerable – for example, if a drought destroys a whole crop of rice. The strength (and honesty) of the government in LEDCs as well as the conscience of businesses in developed economies determines whether LEDCs benefit or lose out from international trade.

Talking Point

What do you think governments in LEDCs should do to prevent the possibility of their economies being exploited?

Revision Essentials

Exporting – **selling products produced in one country to customers in another country.**

Importing – **buying products produced in another country.**

Less economically developed country (LEDC) – **a country that has a relatively low standard of living and lacks the capacity to produce manufactured goods.**

Trade – **when economies begin to benefit from exchanging goods with each other.**

Exercises

(A and B: 12 marks; 25 minutes)

A1. Describe the meaning of the term 'trade'. (2)

2. Explain two benefits of trade to a less economically developed country. (4)

3. Explain two potential costs of trade to a less economically developed country. (4)

B   In 2009 the EU gave LEDCs such as Jamaica the right to sell bananas to member countries above the market price in order to benefit their producers. However, any aim to reduce poverty was unfulfilled as those in the LEDCs felt little benefit. Instead, banana distributors such as Fyffes captured much of the inflated price without passing it down to producers.

Adapted from: *The Financial Times*, 18 December 2009

1. Bananas are classified as a commodity product. Which two of the following are also classified as commodities: (2)

a)   Televisions

b)   copper

c)   rice

d)   tyres?

2. Explain why setting the price the EU would pay for the bananas might help countries such as Jamaica. (4)

Classroom Activity

(Groups of 4; 30 minutes)

In groups of four collect together six items such as clothing, stationery, food, mobile phones, etc. Try to find out who makes them and where in the world they are made.

On a wall in your classroom you could create a world map and show where some of your group's products are imported from.

Practice Questions

Questions

(15 marks; 30 minutes)

1   Which of the following is *not* a benefit to the UK of trading with other counties? (1)

a) The UK will be able to access prodcts that cannot be produced in Britain.

b) There may be cheaper products because there is increased competition.

c) As more products are imported, the number of people employed in the UK in manufacturing has fallen.

d) Exporting products to other countries can help to stimulate economic growth.

2 The table shows the value of exports and imports of the top five commodity exporting LEDCs in 2007.

Merchandise exports and imports of the least-developed countries by selected country grouping, 2007

	Exports		Imports	
	Value (million $)	Annual percentage change	Value (million $)	Annual percentage change
	2007	2000–07	2007	2000–07
Zambia	4619	32	3971	22
Mozambique	2700	33	3300	16
Congo, Dem. Rep. of	2650	18	3700	27
Tanzania	2022	16	5337	20
Senegal	1698	9	4452	17

Source: WTO, World Trade Developments in 2007.

1 Explain the meaning of the term 'commodity'. Give two examples of commodities that might be exported by the countries in the table (4)

2 State which country has the largest difference between the value of their commodity exports and their imports. (2)

3 Zambia is keen to develop its exports to continue to help their development. However, relying too heavily on commodity products can be risky.

To what extent is it certain that an increase in the value of exports will lead to an increase in the standard of living in Zambia? (8)

Chapter 32

Trade restrictions

In 2004, the Brazilian Government claimed that between 1999 and 2003 the US Government gave $12.5bn to its cotton farmers. This means that US farmers are able to sell their cotton much cheaper because the government handout covers any losses made. So although Brazilian farmers (and those in West Africa) can make cotton cheaper, people prefer to buy cotton from the US because the government handout means they sell it for less than Brazilians (and West Africans) can.

By supporting their farmers to carry on producing cotton even though they are not the most ideal to do it, the US Government is restricting trade. In theory, Americans should import cotton from Brazil and West Africa, and US workers should produce what they are good at. But the US Government knows that several thousand people are employed in cotton farming in America and so it prefers to support the industry rather than see these people become unemployed and have to re-train.

The US Government *could* say that it is their right to decide how to spend US taxpayers' money. Remember, though, that the average American is 20 times richer than the average West African. So, it does seem morally wrong for richer American farmers to be given subsidies that stop Africans making a living.

How can trade be restricted?

Countries have a variety of **trade barriers** available that make it difficult for other countries to get their products into their economy. These are:

1 *Tariffs*: A **tariff** is a tax on importing goods into a country. In September 2009 the US government put a 55 per cent tax on tyres imported from China. This means that if a Chinese company charged $25 for a tyre, a US customer would have to pay $38.75 for it. The extra $13.75 would go to the US Government.

2 *Quotas*: A **quota** is a limit on the amount of an item that can be imported over a period of time. Once the limit has been reached, no more will be allowed in until the following time period. A quota system is soon to be applied to Premier League footballers, preventing too many overseas players from playing in Britain.

3 *Subsidies*: Governments can provide **subsidies** to their own producers so that they can charge less for their products than it would cost to import them. This approach penalises foreign producers as effectively as an import tariff.

4 *Non-tariff barriers*: Governments can deliberately make it difficult to engage in trade. Importing can be made difficult by:

- checking every item being brought through every port and airport
- demanding complicated paperwork
- making products conform to standards that are costly to meet.

Why do countries restrict trade?

Putting up trade barriers is called **protectionism** because it defends (protects) the home economy. There are several reasons why a government may engage in protectionism:

1 *Not having to compete with firms in other economies means that jobs are more secure at home.* The EU supports its farmers from cheaper food available in other countries by providing them with subsidies. Without these subsidies many thousands of farmers would be out of work and failure to protect jobs would make the government unpopular.

2 *New industries may be able to compete in the future but while they are growing they need protection from larger competitors abroad.* Once they have grown, the protectionism can be removed.

3 *An economy may believe that it needs its own supply of a particular good at all times.* A country will not want to rely on another country for food, energy or military equipment in case relations take a turn for the worse in the future.

4 *Some industries are closely linked to national tradition.* Keeping them in business by protecting them is seen as necessary for national pride.

The Science Bit

The World Trade Organisation (WTO) tries to promote *free trade.* This would mean that every economy would benefit from trade because there would be no restrictions. The WTO resolves disputes between countries and has the power to impose fines on members who rely on protectionist measures.

Conclusion

Free trade should, in theory, benefit everyone because goods will be provided at the lowest cost possible. However, governments are often tempted to put barriers in the way of free trade in order to benefit their own economy at the expense of another. However, protectionism from one economy usually leads to retaliation, and the world economy as a whole loses out.

Talking Point

What factors do you think make protectionism more likely?

Revision Essentials

Free trade – **there are no barriers to trade between two economies.**

Protectionism **– using trade barriers to shield companies in your economy from international competition.**

Quota **– a limit on the number of goods that can be imported.**

Trade subsidy **– a handout given to home producers to make imported goods uncompetitive.**

Tariff **– a tax on the import of goods.**

Trade barrier **– a measure used by one country to make it less attractive to import goods from other countries.**

Exercises

(A and B: 13 marks; 30 minutes)

A1. **Match the type of trade restriction to its description in the table below.** (3)

Tariffs	A limit on the number of a product or service that is allowed into a country.
Quotas	Introduced by a country to make it hard for a business to export their products to that country. This might include complex regulations and time-consuming documentation and paperwork.
Non-tariff barriers	This is a tax on a good or service when it enters a country. This tax makes the price more expensive and so the product is less competitive and so sales will fall.

B   Fishing counts for 6 per cent of Iceland's economic activity (and 70 per cent of its exports). Iceland is famous for its more sustainable approach to fishing. However, cheaper imports from Spanish fishing businesses are threatening the jobs of Icelandic fishermen.

1.   Explain why Iceland would consider introducing trade restrictions. (4)

2.   State which trade restriction you believe is most appropriate to protect Iceland's fishermen. Explain your answer. (6)

Classroom Activity

(Groups of 3 or 4; 45 minutes)

In groups, use the internet to find out about two countries that China has imposed trade restrictions on. Prepare to describe these examples and explain why you think the trade restrictions are in place.

Practice Questions

In August 2009 the increase in unemployment was the highest since 1995. The manufacturing sector was hit particularly hard. The UK was also importing more than it exported. Unemployed people found it difficult to accept cheap imports filling shelves while they were out of work.

Workers and their union representatives put pressure on the Government to create trade barriers in order to protect jobs.

Questions

(16 marks; 30 minutes)

1   Describe two ways in which the Government could reduce imports. (4)

2   To what extent do you believe restricting trade will have long-term benefits for a country such as the UK? (8)

3   Apart from protectionist measures, describe a strategy that the UK Government could follow to support industry in Britain. (4)

Chapter 33

Single European Market

In 2007 Bulgaria and Romania joined the **European Union** (EU), taking the total number of countries to 27. Both countries had to make lots of preparations to be allowed to join the EU. Why were they so determined to do so?

What is a single market?

The European Union provides common goals on things like human rights and international security but its primary objective is to provide a **single market.**

Before the EU each country's economy operated completely independently. Germany may have traded freely with Austria but not with Sweden. When joining the European Single Market, the member countries are allowing their economies to operate 'as one' with the other members. Each member economy is just part of the larger EU economy.

This means that there are no restrictions on trade and movement between any of the countries. For example:

- goods moving between member countries are very rarely checked at borders, thus speeding up the process. There are no tariffs or quotas between countries in the EU
- any safety, specification or qualification standards are the same across all the countries. So, a TV produced in Hungary is 'fit' for sale in Portugal, and workers from one country have

the right to work in another member country because their qualifications are recognised.

In 1999 the EU went one step further to making the individual economies function as one larger one when they introduced the Euro. The Euro is a **single currency** used by 16 of the EU members. Not having to exchange money to trade with other countries removed the remaining barrier to trade between member countries. If a German company buys from a French supplier, there is no risk that a change in the exchange rate will cause an unexpected increase in price. But if the German firm buys from Britain (outside the Euro), a rise in the pound can increase the price to be paid by the German firm. So why take the risk? Why not buy from France and forget about Britain?

How the EU can improve standards of living

Removing any potential barriers to trade should improve standards of living. The reasons for this are that:

- the single currency means that it is clear if you are paying too much for something in your country compared with another, so you are more likely to get the best deal. This means that people can afford more items to improve their standard of living

- no trade restrictions means there are 350 million customers to sell to, potentially increasing sales and income and reducing unemployment. Also, the variety of items available across the EU means customers get more choice

- workers can move to economies with higher wages so they can afford more items to improve their standard of living.

The Science Bit

European firms have to be able to compete with economic giants such as America, China and Japan. This could be difficult if a company is operating in an economy such as France or Britain, with a much smaller population. Grouping the countries of Europe together into a single market provides a chance of competing with these giants. Selling BMW Minis to the 350-million population of Europe makes it easier to achieve economies of scale such as bulk-buying. Having reduced costs per car to the minimum, it is then easier for the Mini to compete with Japanese or US car producers.

Conclusion

As of 2009, the European Single Market is a collection of 27 economies. They effectively operate as one larger economy because there are no restrictions on the movement of goods and people between them. The complete lack of restrictions means that everyone benefits from free trade and, as a result, the standard of living should increase.

Talking Point

To what extent do you think the increases in standard of living since the EU was formed are due to the single market and not the EU's work on human rights, education and infrastructure?

Revision Essentials

European Union – Europe's single market, with 27 members.

Single currency – a way to improve the effectiveness of a single market by removing the trade barrier of currency exchange.

Single market – a group of economies that agree to act as one larger economy with no restriction on trade between the members.

Exercises

(A and B: 20 marks; 40 minutes)

A1. State three benefits an economy may receive as a result of being in the Single European Market. (3)

2. Explain how increased trade may impact on economic growth in a member country. (4)

3. The chart shows the amount of trade occurring between member states in the European Union (EU).

a) How much of Germany's trade is done with countries outside the EU? (1)

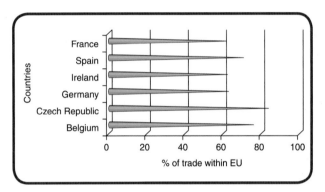

Trade within the EU

Source: www.europa.eu

b) Suggest and explain one reason why the percentage of the Czech Republic's trade within the EU is higher than the other countries. (4)

B   A survey by a leading research organisation looked at how people in the countries joining the EU in 2004 felt about joining the Single European Market. They found out that three in every four people felt that joining would improve their job and training prospects and improve opportunities. However, the survey also mentioned their concerns that joining would lead to increases in local prices. They felt that Europe was already an expensive place to live and that this would be 'passed on' to their countries once they joined.

Source: Market Research World.

1. Explain how increased trading opportunities would help to raise the standard of living in countries joining the Single European Market. (4)

2. Explain how price rises would have an impact on the standard of living. (4)

Classroom Activity

(Groups of 2; 40 minutes)

In pairs, you will be given the name of one or two member countries of the Single European Market. Produce a fact sheet about them. The fact sheet should include information on:

- population
- GDP
- GDP per capita (per person in the country)
- currency
- imports and exports (what do they import/export and how much?)
- Human Development Index (this helps to give you an idea about standard of living).

When you put this together with the rest of the class you will have a picture of the different nations that make up the Single European Market. Use this as a discussion point with your classmates about standard of living.

Practice Questions

A single market provides free movement of goods, services, money and people. When Poland and seven other eastern European counties joined the Single European Market in 2004, they expected increases in standards of living.

A report in *The Independent* in July 2009 discussed the effect of the extra eight members of the Single European Market on the UK. It said that workers who came to Britain from eastern Europe to live and work have made a positive economic contribution and that they have paid 37 per cent more in taxes than any benefits they have received. It was also reported that immigrants were, on average, younger, better educated and highly more skilled than the domestic population. They would also work for much lower wages and take jobs that many Britons wouldn't.

Questions

(9 marks; 20 minutes)

1 Explain how the movement of workers from eastern Europe to Britain could have a positive impact on the UK's economy. (3)

2 In 2007, Romania and Bulgaria also joined the Single European Market. However, there were temporary restrictions on the free movement of their people into other existing member countries. Explain why you think these restrictions were put in place. (6)

Chapter 34

Multinational organisations

In 2009, the Volkswagen group had 61 production factories in twenty-one countries around the world. These facilities provide employment for over 350,000 people, and can produce nearly 30,000 vehicles a day. Having a presence in so many countries makes Volkswagen a **multinational** organisation.

Volkswagen's headquarters are in Wolfsburg, Germany. In theory, the group could have one huge factory in Germany that produces all the cars and vans. The finished vehicles would then be sent to the 150 or so countries they sell to across the globe.

However, there are many reasons why Volkswagen choose to produce cars in factories around the world:

1. *Reduction in transport costs.* Moving bulky items such as cars and vans is expensive. Producing nearer to customers means that they have to be transported less far. Volkswagen will also consider how far the factory is from raw materials when picking a location.

2. *Lower costs.* Wages in less economically developed countries (LEDCs) are lower than in developed ones. Also, land may be cheaper and regulation may be more relaxed, which means fewer costs to pay on rent and complying with health and safety laws.

3. *Avoiding trade barriers.* Producing cars in the country in which they are bought may be cheaper than importing them into a country due to tariffs. For example, Japanese electronics firms face import tariffs when importing televisions, computers and hi-fis into the European Union (EU). To avoid this, they set up factories inside the EU.

How multinationals can help LEDCs

Multinational organisations can benefit LECDs because they provide:

- *Employment.* Multinational organisations provide jobs and income for the population of LEDCs. This income can improve the standard of living of the population, especially when it is spent on purchasing goods produced in the LEDC.

- *Training.* Being in employment in a multinational will provide workers with valuable training and education that could be transferable to other businesses. When the workforce becomes more skilled, other multinationals may be tempted to set up in the LEDC, or local people could choose to set up their own businesses.

- *Investment.* Multinationals can contribute to improving the local infrastructure. They may offer to pay for improvements to transport or communication systems. They are paying because they need these improvements, but they will benefit the community as a whole.

- *Tax revenue.* Workers' wages and the multinational's profits will be subject to tax in the LEDC. If this money is collected, it can be put towards improving infrastructure for everyone.

- don't care about the environment. There may be very few laws to prevent overuse of resources such as water or the dumping of waste in LEDCs, and multinationals can exploit this situation.

How multinationals can damage LEDCs

Multinationals are often criticised for damaging the LEDCs they choose to locate in. The criticisms are that they:

- reserve well-paid jobs for people brought in from their own country. This means that local workers' career prospects are more limited than would otherwise be the case.

- withdraw profit and pay very little tax. Clever accountants can ensure that very little tax is paid, and that profits made are sent back to the home country or – more likely – to an offshore tax haven such as Bermuda where no tax is charged.

- are very footloose. Multinationals can be tempted by large financial incentives and when these run out they may pack up and move to another country. They may show little or no loyalty to their staff.

Conclusion

Businesses choose to set up in several countries because it can give them an advantage over a rival who chooses to operate from one central base. A company that does this is called a multinational. A multinational can bring several benefits to, but can also damage, the economies of LEDCs. The extent to which multinationals make a positive overall contribution depends on how responsible the business is and how strong the government is in the LEDC.

Talking Point

If you were the leader of the government of a LEDC, would you provide subsidies to encourage a multinational to set up in your country? If so, why and, if not, then why not?

Revision Essentials

Multinational – an organisation that has facilities (offices, factories, etc.) in several countries.

Exercises

(A and B: 25 marks; 40 minutes)

A1. In your own words describe what makes a business a 'multinational'. Give two examples of companies that are multinationals. (3)

2. Explain how multinationals contribute to globalisation. (4)

3. Describe two reasons why a business might want to become a multinational. (4)

4. Explain three problems that multinationals can bring to the countries where they locate. (6)

B   Coca-Cola is the global leader in soft drinks. Established in 1886, they have production facilities in 120 countries and have more than 3,000 products.

Source: www.thecoca-colacompany.com

1. Explain why Coca-Cola prefers to have bases in so many different countries, rather than operating from just a few (or even one). (4)

2. Suggest two steps that Coca-Cola could take to reduce any negative impact of expanding into another country. (4)

Classroom Activity

(Groups of 2–3; 40 minutes)

The website www.corporatewatch.org.uk contains a range of information about multinational businesses.

Work in pairs to research a chosen business and prepare a brief presentation or report, highlighting what impact this business is having on a country that it has chosen to locate in.

Practice Questions

The UK is the sixth largest economy in the world and the largest investor in foreign countries.

Most UK multinational companies have glossy brochures showcasing their socially responsible work and the activities that they undertake. However, one view is that much of this is at a surface level, concentrating on planting trees and cutting the use of electricity. There is little focus on the social and environmental impacts of the businesses.

Adapted from: Guardian.co.uk, 21 March 2004

Tesco operates in the following countries:

- UK
- Ireland
- Hungary
- Czech Republic
- Slovakia
- Poland
- China
- India
- South Korea
- Japan
- Thailand
- Malaysia
- USA.

Source: www.tescoplc.com

Questions

(15 marks; 35 minutes)

1 Which of the following is *not* a reason why a business would want to become a multinational? (1)

a) It is easy to set up.

b) They may avoid trade barriers.

c) It may spread risk.

d) It reduces transport costs.

2 Explain three reasons why Tesco has chosen to locate in so many countries across the globe. (6)

3 Analyse the impact that a large multinational business could have on the lives and environments of people in less economically developed countries. (8)

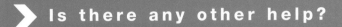
Chapter 35

International government

In 2009 the American and Chinese Governments played 'chicken' over the issue of global warming. Although both knew there would be benefits from a joint plan to cut CO_2 emissions, they competed to try to force the other country to act first. After nine months of conflict China set a target of cutting the 'intensity' of its greenhouse gas emissions by 45 per cent by 2020. America quickly followed by promising to cut 2020 emissions by 17 per cent compared with a 2005 baseline.

Why was it a struggle? Why didn't they work together? The same principle can be scaled up to more than two governments. Helping out the world's poor has costs for richer governments but if all governments did the same, the costs and benefits would be shared. However, individual governments fear that if they help, others will not and that they will then be bearing all the costs.

Each government is motivated by pleasing those who elected them. In the main, their electorate prefers their own job security and wealth to that of people in developing countries. This means that governments act in their own short-term interests at the expense of those living in poverty in other countries.

Perhaps there is a need for a system of **international government** that can encourage countries to cooperate. They might even penalise those that don't (or at least prevent them from sharing the rewards).

What international government exists?

- The United Nations has a Department of Economic and Social Affairs that focuses on improving standards of living, improving welfare and reducing poverty. It gathers data and organises meetings to help members make decisions on how to reduce poverty.

- The World Trade Organisation (WTO) attempts to promote trade between countries. Historically, developing countries have missed out from the benefits of trade, as richer countries have preferred to trade with each other. The WTO's primary focus is to encourage governments to reduce trade barriers so that all countries can benefit from trade. It also resolves situations where two countries cannot agree on trade issues.

The G8 is a collection of the world's richest (but not biggest) eight economies. They meet to discuss issues that require collective action, such as poverty and climate change. The G8+5 also includes South Africa, China, India, Mexico and Brazil, a group that includes some of the world's fastest-growing economies.

Does international government work?

Each international government institution has had its relative successes. The WTO has resolved trade disputes that would have otherwise damaged developing economies. The G8 has been involved in writing off much of the debt owed to it by the developing world, and increased the amount of aid.

However, in contrast the most recent round of trade negotiations run by the WTO has run for nine years without any sign of agreement. The problem is the same: individual governments are unwilling to give anything up unless they are assured others are doing the same. Of course, opinions on what is equal and what is not are hard to come by. The result is that progress on creating a fairer world is incredibly slow.

The Science Bit

The most recent round of trade negotiations organised by the WTO is called the Doha round (named after where the first meeting was held). The most common sticking point in negotiations is rules regarding agriculture. In America farmers have an influential voice in the government and are given preferential treatment. As a result even though America should leave cotton farming to developing economies like Brazil (as they can do it cheaper) the US Government keeps farmers happy by offering them subsidies. This puts poorer Brazilian farmers at a disadvantage. The last thing the US Government would want to do is give this up (and annoy its farmers) without something in return.

Conclusion

In theory international government would make sure that individual governments would act in everyone's collective interest. The reality is that individual governments focus on improving the quality of life for those in their own country. When attempts are made at international cooperation, it is often painfully slow. Perhaps international government organisations need more powers to force cooperation. In Britain, people are worried about Europe having too much power. It is hardly likely that voters would accept the idea of a World Government having even more power over our lives.

Talking Point

Would you be in favour of a stronger international government with the ability to punish those who don't cooperate?

Revision Essentials

International government – **organisations that try to coordinate the efforts of individual governments.**

Exercises

(A and B: 17 marks; 35 minutes)

A1. State three reasons why a developed country such as the US might help a poorer country. (3)

2. The example outlined in 'The Science Bit' of this chapter explains how the US might not always act in the best interests of developing countries. Describe two reasons why a country such as Britain might also act against the best interests of poorer countries. (4)

B An article in The Guardian stated: 'Without a willingness by the West to bankroll greener economic strategies in the developing world there will be no climate change deal.'

Source: *The Guardian*, 9 November 2009, http://www.guardian.co.uk/business/2009/nov/09/bank-tax-pays-for-development

This article highlights a very real problem: rising emissions of greenhouse gasses by developing countries, but too little cash to afford the technology to make the burning of fossil fuels more environmentally friendly.

1. Why do developed countries have a motive to support the purchase of these new expensive technologies? (4)

2. Explain why people who live in rich countries might not support government aid being given to poorer countries. (6)

Classroom Activity

(Groups of 4; 30 minutes)

Oxfam states that 'Over 23 million people across East Africa are facing critical shortages of food and water following successive years of failed rains and worsening drought.'

Working in groups of four, discuss the costs and benefits of the UK helping an East African country such as Somalia. Produce a mind-map to show your thoughts, and be ready to talk these through with the rest of the class.

Practice Questions

The following comment was posted on *The Scotsman* newspaper website following the G8 summit in Gleneagles, from a US web-user.

Charity begins at home.
ALL foreign aid should cease at once so that the American taxpayers are taken care of.
If the Centre for Global Development bunch of busybodies wants to contribute to the world's poor let them go ahead and knock themselves out, but let them do it with their own money.
http://news.scotsman.com

Questions

(10 marks; 20 minutes)

To what extent do you agree with this statement? Use your knowledge about the motives and consequences of providing aid to poorer countries to support your answer. (10)

Chapter 36

Charities and NGOs

On Saturday 2 July 2005, rock and pop stars from around the world took part in ten concerts collectively titled 'Live8'. Three billion people were reported to have watched the concerts either live or on TV. The '8' from Live8 refers to the G8, the name given to the eight richest countries in the world. The concerts were charitable events, designed to raise awareness of 'Make Poverty History'. This campaigning organisation was created to pressurise richer governments to send more aid to, and cancel debts owed by, poor counties. Shortly after the Live8 campaign, the UK (and others) cancelled many of the debts and modestly increased the amount of aid to the world's poorest.

Charities and Non-Governmental Organisations (NGOs)

Several **charities** and **Non-Governmental Organisations** (NGOs) such as Make Poverty History, Free Trade, Oxfam, ActionAid and Voluntary Service Overseas (VSO) work on an international scale to try to reduce poverty. Charities are run by trustees and are financed by public donations. NGOs are private organisations, but often enjoy some government funding. Both are not-for-profit and use any financial surpluses to promote the interests of the poor (and the environment) and relieve suffering.

Their work can be broken down into three approaches:

- campaigning among the population, businesses and governments of richer countries to donate money that can be used to provide aid to those in poor countries

- campaigning to businesses and governments (both rich and poor) to change what they do in order to protect and support the poorest.

- providing opportunities for those in richer countries to work as volunteers to help poor communities abroad.

Can they reduce world poverty?

Charities and NGOs have no legal power. They cannot change laws or force richer countries to trade with poor ones. Their success is dependent on the pressure they can put on individuals and governments to donate or make changes in order to reduce poverty.

Donating money or time to those in need should never be discouraged but it is often criticised for being a temporary solution. Donations of food or money may help in the short term but for poverty to be reduced over the long term any attempts must be sustainable. Once their immediate health is secure, aid must provide the poor with means of pulling themselves out of poverty in the long term. This might include offering very small loans (known as micro-loans) for setting up small enterprises, or providing equipment and livestock for farming.

The famous Mother Teresa once said: 'I want the fishing rod, not the fish.' In other words a fish keeps a family alive for a day, but a fishing rod could help the family keep itself alive for the future.

Charities and NGOs can have their biggest impact on poverty if they convince governments to change how they behave.

For example, the Fairtrade NGO has persuaded several businesses to ensure that the producers of their food get a fair deal. In 2009 Cadbury began to make its Dairy Milk range from Fairtrade Cocoa. For every ton of cocoa that Cadbury buys (15,000 tonnes a year) it must pay a minimum price high enough to help support the livelihoods of farming communities.

However, the work of charities and NGOs can easily be undone if governments aren't strong enough to protect the poor. In 2007 one US soldier was convicted of accepting $10m worth of bribes in return for allocating aid money to chosen contractors. Clearly, a lot of poverty in developing countries could be prevented by fairer and/or stronger government and until this is the case, charities and NGOs are, to some extent, fighting a losing battle.

Conclusion

Charities and NGOs can play a significant role in reducing poverty. For example, Live8 and Fairtrade have made a valuable contribution to reducing debt and increasing aid. However, their success is limited by two factors: the degree to which the support is sustainable and the strength of the government in making sure that support gets to where it is most needed.

Talking Point

Do you think Cadbury used Fair Trade cocoa for its Dairy Milk range solely in order to reduce world poverty?

Revision Essentials

Charities – organisations committed to raising awareness and money for a cause such as world poverty.

Non-Governmental Organisations – not-for-profit organisations that are separate from government and set up to promote the interests of the poor (and the environment) and relieve their suffering.

Exercises

(A and B: 18 marks; 35 minutes)

A1. In your own words, describe the difference between a charity and a Non-Governmental organisation. Use two examples to illustrate your answer. (4)

2. Explain two reasons why a charity might have limited effect when trying to support the population of a developing country. (6)

B   A report produced in June 2008 by a team of health economists suggested that up to half of the funding for children and teenagers' National Health Service (NHS) cancer centres comes from charities. Top doctors even argued that without the support from these charities many of these centres would not exist.

Adapted from: BBC News, 20 June 2008

1. Discuss whether the NHS should have to rely on charities to provide these facilities. (8)

Classroom Activity

(Groups of 3 or 4; 30 minutes)

Oxfam Unwrapped allows people to purchase gifts to help others in developing counties. For example, for £25 you can buy a goat, or for £8 you can buy some schoolbooks.

Other charities such as the Red Cross prefer general donations that are then spent according to need.

In your group discuss both options and why Oxfam have preferred their 'unwrapped' gift strategy. Think about the impact each option can have in the developing world.

For more information, go to: www.oxfam.org.uk/unwrapped.

Practice Questions

Questions

(15 marks; 30 minutes)

'Corruption is an issue which affects both rich and poor countries, but it is the poorest people who suffer most from it. We believe corruption must be tackled in order to make poverty history.'

Adapted from: Make Poverty History website, http://www.makepovertyhistory.org

1 Explain how fear of corruption could change the charity-giving habits of people in rich countries. (3)

2 Analyse how corruption can affect the impact that aid has on the lives of populations in developing countries. (4)

3 Should rich countries continue to provide aid even when the government of a less-developed economy is believed to be corrupt? Explain your answer. (8)

Index